Toward a Philosophy of Praxis

Toward a Philosophy of Praxis

Karol Wojtyla

(POPE JOHN PAUL II)

AN ANTHOLOGY EDITED BY
ALFRED BLOCH AND GEORGE T. CZUCZKA

CROSSROAD · NEW YORK

1981
The Crossroad Publishing Company
18 East 41st Street, New York, N.Y. 10017

Library of Congress Cataloging in Publication Data

John Paul II, Pope, 1920–
Toward a philosophy of praxis.

1. Catholic Church—Collected works. 2. Theology —Collected works—20th century. I. Bloch, Alfred, 1922– II. Czuczka, George T. III. Title.
BX1751.2.J64 230'.2 80-21239
ISBN 0-8245-0033-4
Previously: 0-8164-0463-1

Printed in the United States of America

Contents

INTRODUCTION

Karol Wojtyla: The Power of Words

KAROL WOJTYLA, as John Paul II, brings to the papacy a personality shaped by the unique historical tradition of a select group of Poles known within Poland as the "intelligentsia" because of its common fight for freedom of spirit, conscience, and national identity. It is also known for its conceit, disregard of social conventions, and drive to play for often unnecessarily dangerous stakes.

Since the late eighteenth century, while their Western European counterparts' expression was restrained only by conventional mores, Polish intellectuals worked in somber, conspiratorial obscurity haunted by police, repressed by fawning politicians, and frequently liquidated. If they made their work public at all, they did so as emigrés. Chopin, for example, could not play his music in Poland, but in leaving Poland he was able to make a gift of the mazurkas and the polonaise to the world. But most others remained obscure, known only to a handful of specialized scholars.

Although Polish thought did not have the wider recognition it deserved, the intelligentsia had power at least within Poland, insofar as they carefully used the "Word" to express faith in their nation, their God, and their irrepressibly idealistic conviction that a just cause must win. This idealism, however, has been well anchored in the most difficult and complex *realpolitik*—the politics of permanent opposition.

In the context of constraint and obscurantism, conspiracy acquires a special meaning. First, it is a moral stance, and its morality is absolute. Secondly, it demands solidarity and a high degree of personal responsibility. Thirdly, it needs the support of the masses who may have been misled to side with their oppressors. Those who engage in conspiratorial politics know that they run the risk of failure, oblivion and worse. Armed only with words, they must be imaginative, flexible, and supremely adept at focusing on the total picture. A long history of trial and error has taught the Polish intelligentsia what strategy to employ and how much pressure to apply. The aim is to confound the authoritarian system in question to the point of toppling it and then to wait patiently for it to fall, while continuing to convey to the people the message of hope, faith, and reason.

Karol Wojtyla remains a major representative of the Polish intelligentsia. But now that he is pope, his forum has greatly expanded. The values shaped in conspiratorial opposition for which he stands and the "Word" he speaks are now heard in the four corners of the world.

Since assuming the pontificate, John Paul II has been moving along the path he charted in the writings from which we shall quote with determination, vigor, and, above all, with unwavering dedication to fundamentals. But the common enemy now, he seems to be saying, is more subtle. He is this man here and that woman there; he is you and—if we look closely—he is I. The enemy is or may be each and every one of us, living in this time, subject to these present-day stresses, buffeted by all the forces we have unleashed in the name of civilization, and sorely beset by the seven deadly sins.

The enemy opposes us on the battleground of the everyday life we share with our equally harassed fellow men; he invades the private life we lead with our loved ones; he places obstacles between men who were created in the image of God; and he will, on occasion, intrude upon our dreams and leave us bereft when we awake.

This fear of fear itself, the condition we know so well by the name of anxiety in the modern world, has caused not a few to throw in their lot with conformist systems and regimented ideologies in the hope of finding relief, security, and perhaps even a sense of purpose. It is in response to this temptation that the enemy takes on intellectual and social form in the "two materialisms," which in the nineteenth and twentieth centuries have captured the imaginations of so many.

Marxist materialism, on one hand, calls for a reorganization of society to permit collective interests to dominate social activity—a course Marx himself said would lead to the formation of "true consciousness." As the history of this century has amply demonstrated, his ideas have been misinterpreted, to say the least, by those who came to power in his name. They have used his notion of the role of the collective as the primary rationalization to imprison any individual exhibiting non-conformism to state ideology.

Capitalist materialism, on the other hand, assigns the topmost role to the individual and his private interests, and envisions the world as a vast competitive arena in which the winner takes all and the loser, more often than not, falls victim to exploitation and alienation.

Both forms of materialism, even when tempered by an infusion of liberalism, have produced a terrifying heap of destroyed human lives. The two catastrophic world wars which killed and maimed more than one hundred million people, the narcissism of the West, the debilitating enforced conformism of the East, and the universal fixation with national security and escalating armaments at the expense of human priorities all attest to it.

To avert disaster, we have been trying to crossbreed the two materialisms, but we do not really believe that this balancing act between the needs of the individual and those of the collective will succeed. The attempts to find a unifying symbol, to achieve convergence, or at least accommodation, cannot bear fruit because fundamental human value structures remain unchanged and because the spiritual dimension and the spiritual needs of humanity go ignored.

John Paul's task in unmasking the enemy and expanding consciousness is a creative process which builds on itself. His fundamental strategy as pope, similar to his strategy in Poland, is to use the "Word." For him the battle ground is language. In describing the sin of Adam and Eve he says,

> The evil spirit is recognizable and identifiable not by means of some definition of his being, but solely from the contents of his words. Here, in the third chapter of Genesis, at the very beginning of the Bible, it becomes clear that the history of mankind, and with it the history of the world with which man is united through the work of divine creation, will both be subject to the rule of the Word and the anti-Word, the Gospel and the anti-Gospel.

John Paul found the "Word," the language of the heart we too must learn if we are to overcome the "Anti-Word," in the Gospel; he found it in the writings of the Church Fathers, St. Augustine and

St. Thomas, in the ecstatic visions of St. John of the Cross, and in those of secular thinkers—in Marx, in the somberly devout poetry of Cyprian Norwid, a 19th century Polish expatriate, and in the discourses of the German philosopher Max Scheler, a sometime Catholic and sometime phenomenologist. John Paul wrote his doctoral dissertation on St. John of the Cross and did original research on Scheler, whose work is still largely unknown in America.

Although the influence of St. Thomas shines through all the writings of Karol Wojtyla, the impact of Max Scheler adds a very dramatic and contemporary flavor to Karol Wojtyla's philosophy. Scheler viewed the world of the twenties much as concerned humanists view it today. In 1921, a year after Karol Wojtyla was born, Scheler observed that few ages in history rejected religious values more universally and more heedlessly than his own. At the same time, he said, "few ages have had a keener presentiment of a turning point, a break with the outworn; a radical break with a culture hostile to religion."

Karol Wojtyla lived through two of the worst dictatorships of contemporary history, Hitlerism and Stalinism, both of which were comparable in content, horror, and intent. Both "benefited" from technology in ways which no one can be proud. Looking at this technology Max Scheler said in 1926 that, "even if positive science should be completed, man as a spiritual being would still be completely empty. In fact he might relapse into barbarism." This is what happened and Scheler prophesied that this barbarism when "supported systematically by science would be the most dreadful of all conceivable barbarisms."

About twenty years separate these words from the gas ovens and cyclonate showers of Auschwitz. Wojtyla was the horror-struck witness of these events. He studied Scheler because he hoped that this perceptive thinker might provide the philosophical foundation for an ethical value structure. But Wojtyla in writing his doctoral dissertation on Scheler's philosophy (mislabeled phenomenology) found it deficient as a model for ethics. Yet the fact remains that Karol Wojtyla has a lasting and all-pervasive interest in philosophical ethics. His original contribution is his insistence that before an ethical value structure can truly be developed, a deeper understanding of the self, of action, of consciousness is required. Insofar as it is possible for the Vicar of Christ on Earth, Wojtyla the philosopher wants to transcend even ethics to be free to explain as clearly as language allows what the self is and how unbelievably precious it is. The uniqueness of the self, the act, and consciousness are all joined into one concept, "the personalistic value of the act."

St. Augustine holds that the soul disposes of three powers which, in their turn, are a reflection of the Trinity in man. The first of the three is the intellect which knows or discovers truth; the second is the will, the love of truth; and the last is memory, to remember truth. These three together are the foundation on which consciousness rests. If consciousness is absent, the individual experiences himself, his fellow men, and the world at some remove; he is a stranger to his own body, a stranger in the midst of his community, an alien presence in the world. Cast adrift, subject to the "perils of the soul," modern man can become and indeed has become the plaything of irrational forces. Consciousness is the armor which protects the religious person against all the demons he might encounter along his way. The Devil, as Pope John Paul II reminds us, has not slept since time began. He is with us now as much as ever.

Religious man must follow the path that has been laid out for him, step by step; he must climb the ladder, rung by rung; and one by one he must confront his devils and demons. And, if he cannot singlehandedly change the whole world, he can bring about a change within himself to set an example for others who will follow his lead. This will happen if his transformation is genuine and if the language he speaks is the language of the heart.

Philosophy was one form through which Karol Wojtyla sought to express the language of the heart, but certainly poetry played an equally important role. The Polish poet who influenced Wojtyla most was Cyprian Norwid. Norwid spent most of his life in exile, because the powers that occupied Poland in the 19th century preferred him there. He sustained himself by writing and painting, but he was not popular even among fellow Polish emigrés, who were somewhat repelled by his strange language and his deep commitment to a rigorist medieval Catholicism too stark for a group accustomed to the easygoing atmosphere of France's Second Empire. He was somber, at times mystical, and strongly committed to a humanity whose future, however, he envisioned as tragic.

But during the short period of Poland's independence (1918-1939) Norwid became a poet's poet, a favorite among a few intellectuals, otherwise still not well known. His works did not really capture the attention of young people until the Nazi occupation of Poland, the time when Wojtyla began his university studies. Wojtyla found in Norwid a kindred spirit whose worldview, shaped under conditions of poverty and repression, was one with which Wojtyla could identify. During the Nazi occupation and throughout the Nazis' ruthless attempts to destroy Polish culture, students who continued to study in underground universities saw in Norwid's poem "Promethidion" a most apt description of prevailing conditions:

Poland!
You are the son of Prometheus
But the vultures devour not your heart—but your brain.

Norwid's Prometheus was not patterned after Greek mythology, but was the symbol of a man who creates himself, creates his humanity through the energy of his thought. It was thought that gave him his human identity.

This theme which recurs inWojtyla's later writings was reinforced by another of Norwid's central perceptions:

Oh History's work is not yet finished
Conscience has not yet burnt its way through the globe.

If anyone were searching for the central theme of John Paul II's pontificate it would have to be his desire to formulate a policy that would make it possible for this conscience to burn "its way through the globe."

Lastly Norwid's prophecy of the future of the world could be John Paul's:

Abundance of all kind will disappear, fade away
Treasures and power will be swept away. . . .
Of the things of this world only two will remain,
Two only: poetry and goodness . . . nothing else.

The poetry Norwid refers to is "The Word" of Wojtyla's reflections and "the goodness" is the work of the Creator.

About the same time that Wojtyla began to identify with the Catholicism and worldview of Norwid, a friend enticed the young man from Wadowice (Wojtyla's birthplace) to join the Rhapsodic

Theater, which performed patriotic pieces during the Nazi occupation and then throughout Stalin's attempts to replace the history of Poland with antilegends suitable to his designs. Under both the Nazis and Stalin the Rhapsodic Theater was an underground organization which held rehearsals and performances on Wednesdays and Saturdays. The theater was a kitchen, a basement, a cold room, and the spot lights were a couple of candles. An audience of twenty was an overflow crowd. The penalty, if they were caught, was either death or exile.

There is a story that Wojtyla at one of the performances given during the Nazi occupation was reciting the lines from *Pan Tadeusz* written by Adam Mickiewicz, Poland's greatest and perhaps most patriotic 19th century poet. In the midst of Wojtyla's performance, the Nazi radio began blaring through loudspeakers an announcement of yet another victory on the Russian front. Wojtyla's strong baritone voice increased in power and displaced the noise of the Nazi victory cry. The lines were:

the night was passing over the milky sky,
the rosy beams of dawn began to fly.

Wojtyla the actor used his voice to fight propaganda and power. In a sense John Paul II standing in the middle of Yankee Stadium telling the poetic story of Lazarus was giving a performance in the same style on a less dangerous though perhaps more deadly stage. The Nazis and the Stalinists tortured and killed human bodies. The enemy in the West that John Paul fights, the culture of narcissism and materialistic greed, leaves the human shell alive while killing the spirit within.

Perhaps the most challenging new role awaiting Karol Wojtyla as papal actor will be that of the "Maximal Rebel." It could be argued that in many ways the integrity and the intensity of the Holy Father's struggle for the recognition of the essential humanness of humanity is very similar to the struggle waged by Albert Camus, the quintessential rebel for humanity. The same forces that shaped Wojtyla brought Albert Camus to develop his themes of opposition or rebellion on behalf of humanity. He led his rebellion from positions very often opposite to those adopted by Karol Wojtyla, but the tone and, in some instances, the content of Camus' rebellion could be Wojtyla's. This becomes especially evident in Camus' book *The Rebel* in which he maintains that:

> There is only one authentic destiny—one that identifies with others. Therefore the individual cannot be by himself alone the embodiment of values he wishes to defend. It needs all humanity to compromise them. When a person rebels he becomes identified with others and so surpasses himself. From this point of view human solidarity can be seen as a metaphysical reality, a truth whose recognition begins with the solidarity born in chains.

In this passage Camus, not unlike Wojtyla, also rejects Scheler, and very much like Wojtyla talks about human fulfillment through an act which results in self-transcendence. John Paul's use of the word "transcend" comes very close to Camus' meaning when he talks of rebelling. The rebellion against conformism, avoidance, degradations of all kinds brought about by Soviet Materialism of mind and Western Materialism of heart is the most dramatic experiential basis of John Paul II's life. For nearly half his adult life he has actively fought against them, and when he accepted the throne of St. Peter, he resumed his rebellion. This is clear in the encyclical *Redemptor Hominis* as well as in the many speeches and homilies he has delivered during his pontificate so far. It is summed up in the title of his retreat talks to the Curia and papal household, the *Sign of Contradiction.*

Camus' rebellion, born of desperation, is the vision of human solidarity in chains. Wojtyla's rebellion is born from the Gospel and the Gospel's evangelical commandment to love. All revolutions, beginning with the one in France in 1789, have promised equality, justice, and fraternity for all, but have mobilized popular energies by creating an atmosphere of hatred, by inflaming popular resentments. Somehow the leaders of these revolutions expected that hatred passing through the crucible of revolution could be transmuted into universal love. But in fact the hatred that mobilized them emerged as a concentrated hatred of the masses and of humanity after the revolution. When this hatred is placed in the hands of a Bonaparte, Hitler, or Stalin, love becomes an illusion. History has proven that to expect love to emerge from hate is either absurd or insane. Wojtyla is challenging us to a different sort of rebellion whose motivating source is genuinely found in love.

The steps in this rebellion begin with the control of certain base drives, then move to the recognition of the importance of every act accomplished by a self, to the realization that participation in the entire human community is the only arena in which each of us will find ultimate fulfillment. This is ultimate rebellion: the quantity of weapons, strategic brilliance, massive organizational capacities, high technology are of no consequence. What counts is our consciousness. It is the rebellion of the magnificence of humanity as quality against the massive insignificance of quantity.

Because of his and our history, because of the narcissism of our culture, and in view of the armaments race that can destroy us all, the Pope could well fulfill the role "maximal rebel." That is a new role for a pope in the theater of the world, and one that is not without danger for both him and the Church he leads.

The world is his audience now; the priests whom he exhorts to preach the Gospel are his troops; and the dogmas of faith he is duty-bound to protect are his principles. He must abide by them and interpret them for a world that changes more rapidly than the human mind can comprehend. He knows that the institutions that gave comfort in the past have become jails for our spirits, but he must also defend these institutions to prevent the dispersion of the enormous energies needed to keep humanity human. He has to consider what to preserve and what to change, what to fight for now and which fight to postpone. That is the greatest challenge confronting him at this moment. If he misjudges he will lose the popular support he needs to win. The pressures and temptations to misjudge are many.

* * *

To acquaint the American reader with the main elements of Karol Wojtyla's thinking, we have selected the core arguments from four major works and the themes to which he consistently returns in all of his writings which are not exclusively devoted to either theology or the administration of the Roman Catholic Church. These works are: "The Theology of the Body,"[1] a still unfinished series of addresses given by John Paul II during his Wednesday general audiences on the relationship between the divine origin of man, love, consciousness, sex, and knowledge; *The Self and the Act,*[2] a plea for human dignity, human values, individuality, solidarity, and human rights; *The Controversy About Man,*[3] a discourse on man's rights and duties toward himself and society; and the *Sign of Contradiction,*[4] a series of meditations on man's encounter with God.

To these excerpts, we have added a summary version of *The Redeemer of Man,*[5] the Pope's first encyclical, and to bring our subject up to date, a number of addresses, homilies, and messages on various subjects, presented on different occasions during the past year.

In providing an English translation of the Pope's writings, an effort was made to achieve clarity and smoothness. Except in the case of official texts, which appear here without change, the translations are quite free—as free, in fact, as we could reasonably make them without taking undue liberties with the original.

Nonetheless, readers may not find the going easy. These texts are not meant merely to be edifying or even inspirational; they do not, as they cannot, provide simple formulas for getting the world back on its tracks or the individual back into his proper mold. In fact, as the Pope said again and again during his pastoral visit to the United States, there are no easy solutions to the many problems we face—there is no easy way out of the dilemma.

NOTES

1. Originally published in *L'Osservatore Romano,* English edition, 19 October 1979 to 16 May 1980. "The Theology of the Body" is our title—ED.

2. Originally published as *Osoba i Czyn* (Krakow: Polskie Towarzystwo Teologiczne, 1969).

3. Originally published as "Osoba: podmiot i wspólnota," in *Roczniki Filozoficzne-Etyka* 24/2, pp. 5–39.

4. *Sign of Contradiction* (New York: The Seabury Press, 1979).

5. *L'Osservatore Romano,* English edition, 19 March 1979.

1

The Individual and Conscious Action: Freedom, Will, Act

> Let us speak, let us speak—
> silence does not suit us,
> since we have been created
> in the image of the word.
> Let us speak, let us speak—
> since within us
> speaks divine thought . . .
>
> C. P. CAVAFY

A MAN of sixty, John Paul II has been a witness to a large part of our century marked by unprecedented manifestations of man's inhumanity to man. He has devoted his life to finding a way back to a humanity which, in Ruysbroeck's words, is "a living mirror in which God has imprinted the image of His nature." To become human in this sense requires, John Paul tells us, faith and a profound philosophical understanding of man as an individual.

The way back is much like a ladder to be laboriously ascended rung by rung from the inferior level of our technological-materialist illusions to a state of consciousness and spiritual maturity which enables us to draw upon our own true inner resources and to resume our rightful place in the divinely structured order of the universe.

During his entire adult life Karol Wojtyla has been refining his understanding of man as he exists, loves, rages, and acts in our time. The two treatises that deal most directly with this theme are The Self and the Act *and* The Controversy about Man. *Both take issue with the Marxist view of man and seek to reestablish the primacy of individual morality as the basis of a moral society.*

Wojtyla clearly and without hesitation asserts his faith over against all other designs invented by man which inevitably lead to the alienation of the self, to misconceived values, and ultimately to a fundamental misunderstanding of what human nature is.

From *The Controversy about Man*

Ours is an age of violent controversy concerning man, the essential meaning of his existence, and, consequently, the nature and value of his being. It is not the first time that Christian philosophy has been confronted by materialist doctrine. But it is the first time that materialism has mustered such a wide variety of resources and expressed itself in so many different ways as it now does in Poland in the political climate spawned by a dialectical Marxism that seeks to capture men's minds. . . . The discussion about man's role in the world over the past twenty years in Poland clearly shows what the heart of the matter is: It is not just a question of cosmology and natural philosophy; it is a question of philosophical anthropology and ethics—it is the great and fundamental contest for the essence of man.

The Subject-Object Experience

Man as a total being, as he stands before us existing and acting, permits us to view him as the subject of his own existence and his own actions. This is the meaning of the term *suppositum,** which seeks to establish man's subjectivity in metaphysical terms. Suppositum or metaphysical subjectivity, the transphenomenal and, for that very reason, fundamental expression of human experience, affirms man's identity in a state of being and action.

To Act and to Be

To comprehend the concept of suppositum, i.e., man's subjectivity in a metaphysical sense, is to grasp the underlying relationship

* "Suppositum," an inspired assumption.—Ed.

between being and action. This relationship is rooted in the philosophical axiom of *operari sequitur esse. . . .* The whole range of human dynamics (*operari* in the widest sense) is determined by what man himself does and brings to pass. The act per se is a specific manifestation of the principle of human *operari*; in the act and through the act man stands revealed as an individual. The true and fundamental meaning of the individual lies first and foremost in the conscious act, which is the expression and consummation of human freedom.

Consciousness and Experience

Consciousness cannot be viewed as a subject in and of itself; but man's personal subjectivity cannot be comprehended without recognizing the central position consciousness occupies. Consciousness is the agent that interiorizes all of man's perceptions—including those perceived within himself as acts of the self—and adds them to the store of personal experience. Man does not become an individual in the truest and fullest sense (i.e., *in actu*) until he experiences himself as an acting (*in actu*) individual.

Self-Determination

The close relationship that exists between a particular person and a particular human act is one of cause and effect. Given this context, authorship of the act in question cannot be detached from one individual and assigned to some other person. The relationship of which we speak is entirely different from the one between man and all the things that simply "happen" to him. Authorship of an act, a conscious act, must therefore be assigned to an individual as its equally conscious author. Such authorship subsumes the concept of freely exercised will and, as a consequence, of moral responsibility. This brings us to the fundamental dimension of man's personal subjectivity.

As one who acts consciously, I am not only the author of the act and its direct and indirect consequences, but also the one who determines himself. Self-determination represents the deeper, more fundamental dimension of human authorship. The synthesis of authorship and self-determination is the only path toward man's revealing himself as an individual endowed with the attributes of self-disposition and self-possession. . . . When man makes a choice between other objects and values, he will inevitably make a determination as to himself and his own value. He thus becomes his own primary object. The structure of the human act is auto-teleological* in a very special sense. . . . Self-determination based on action and rooted in man's authentic authorship points to another dimension of auto-teleology, which itself is contingent on truth and the moral good, the bonum honestum.† This is why transcendence, the second attribute of the individual, is revealed in man's actions.

Self-Fulfillment

Man experiences himself as an individual insofar as he is aware of being in possession of himself and at his own disposition. This experience is conditioned by awareness or rather self-awareness in conjunction with the act itself (authorship as a proximate cause of self-determination). The very fact that the self exhibits a tendency to realize itself is proof of its incompleteness. . . . This tendency rounds out the picture of our self, which takes shape through its own acts performed in awareness and self-awareness. In these acts, the self not only experiences self-possession and self-disposition, but a tendency toward self-fulfillment. In the final analysis, the individual's opening himself completely toward reality has its origin in "turning toward oneself" in awareness and self-awareness. Within the self as a personal subject, self-fulfillment and transcendence are closely intertwined. . . . Let us examine just one aspect of transcendence: the specifically personal imprint that conscience bestows upon the human act. . . . Conscience gives utterance to truth as the origin of moral law (in the "categorical," Kantian sense). This, in turn, is an essential attribute of the freedom associated with the act and with the individual self-determination thereby attained. . . . In this manner, the authentic transcendence of man acting becomes a reality because conscience guides man toward desiring and choosing

* The structure of the human act is in a very special sense "auto-teleological." Every act is an expression of self-determination rooted in a person's authentic authorship of an act. The special aspect of this teleology is its dependence on truth and the moral good.—Ed.

† The bonum honestum is a theological qualification linking truth and the moral good to God's commandments. This is how transcendence, the other necessary quality of the individual, is revealed in his action and in all human action.—Ed.

the "moral good." This, then, is how conscience acts to demonstrate the transcendence of truth and freedom in the act and in its author, the individual. In effect, freedom manifests itself in the desire for and the choice of the moral good. . . . The individual achieves self-fulfillment in the performance of his act provided the act is "good" in itself, i.e., consistent with the dictates of conscience—performed in good or proper conscience, one might add. Through an act such as this, I "become" or "am" a good person. . . . An act contrary to the dictates of conscience, on the other hand, is evil from the standpoint of morality. Through it, I "become" or "am" an evil person. Under such circumstances, the performance of the act does not lead to self-fulfillment. . . . The obvious conclusion to be drawn is that self-fulfillment in the sense of self-realization is not synonymous with performance of the act, but depends upon its moral merit. I cannot attain self-fulfillment merely by performing a given act, but only by performing an act that is morally good. Individual fulfillment is, in fact, predicated upon individual transcendence, i.e., upon the transcendental dimension of the act as objectified by conscience. I am fulfilled by the good; evil, in turn, leads to nonfulfillment, to the extinction of myself as a real person.

From *The Self and the Act*

It is difficult to resist the impression that the number of cognitive efforts directed beyond man far outdistances the sum of all the efforts concentrated on man himself.

Perhaps the reason for this impression lies not only in the number of studies of man, which is quite impressive and specific, but in the fact that man continuously expects new and more penetrating analysis and, above all, desires new synthesis.

The discoverer of so many secrets of nature *must continuously be discovered anew.* He always remains, to a certain degree, an unknown being, demanding increasingly more mature expressions of that being. Moreover, by being the closest and most frequent object of experience, as we have already noted, man is exposed to the danger of becoming commonplace. He runs the risk of becoming common even to himself. This danger also has to be overcome. This can only be achieved by viewing the human being with "awe," and using this awe as the first impulse for cognition of man. This awe, which is not identical with the word "wonder," although wonder is part of it, stands at the beginning of this study. Awe as a function of the intellect turns into a system of questions, which, in turn become a system of answers or solutions. This develops the core of thinking about man and a method of satisfying a specific need of human existence. *Man cannot lose his specific place* within the world he himself formed, which is the world of culture and civilization, or precisely this "contemporary world" over which we labored with so much care and concern as authors of the constitution *Gaudium et spes.*

In a certain way the study we are about to begin relates also to our book *Love and Responsibility,* which was published seven years ago. It was described as "a study in ethics." Although "*The Self and the Act,*" for the above-mentioned reasons, is not a study in ethics, it does have roots in *Love and Responsibility.* In the present study we wish to look at the self for the benefit of the self. We wish to verify the reality of the self on the basis of more elementary and at the same time more universal experiences. It is quite possible that the vision of the self we are attempting to reach will tend to reconfirm in its fashion the correctness of the statements and principles formulated in the ethical study *Love and Responsibility,* but that is not central to our purposes here. The aim of this study is *to reach the understanding of the human self for itself.* Our purpose is to touch human reality at its most appropriate point—at the point that is indicated by human experience and from which man cannot withdraw himself without a feeling that he has lost himself.

The Cognitive Value of the Act

From its very onset our search leads in the direction of recognizing the self through an act, yet we want to emphasize that we are not giving up the superb philosophical intuition that is irreplaceable in the objectification of any dynamism, including the dynamism of a conscious act. Since our goal is the complete and all-inclusive objectification of that dynamism, in as far as that is possible, we will consider and acknowledge all efforts undertaken in that direction, but we will emphasize the function of the act in understanding the self. Only in that way can we bring into full view the reality of the self.

The term act *is identical to* conscious action *and expresses for us the dynamism specific to man as a self.* An act is conscious action. When we say *conscious action,* we affirm through this term that the action is specific to and characteristic of the will. . . . Any specific action of the human will is conscious.

. . . We can see that the term *act* subsumes a wealth of meanings that have to be gradually segregated and explained. The same procedure has to be applied to the gradual unfolding of this reality we identify as the human self.

The Self and the Act is a study conceptualized as a gradual unfolding—"explication" of the "act" in a manner that also unfolds the self. We expect to reach this goal by way of analysis of specific aspects of the act while perpetually keeping in sight the organic integrity of the act in relation to the self.

By describing our conceptualization in this way, we are only following the dictates of logic, because an aspect can neither remove the whole from our view nor replace it. If that were to occur, we would be making one aspect absolute, thereby inaccurately recognizing and reporting a complex reality. The self and the act are a complex reality. The consciousness of complexity and the analytic principles resulting therefrom constantly have to accompany us in our cognitive efforts. While this holds true for an analysis of all complex realities, it is especially important in the analysis of the self, the act, and consciousness.

The term *conscious action* leads us to the aspect of consciousness in the act but does not highlight that aspect. It is therefore necessary to differentiate between conscious action and the consciousness of action. This separation will make it possible to perceive—in a way—consciousness isolated from the act. Through this differentiation we will be able to examine the specific role in the being and acting of the self played by consciousness because *man does not only act consciously but is also conscious of the fact that he is acting consciously.* Yet, in both instances, we use the same term—*conscious/consciously.* However, only one of them is related to consciousness as such.

In our perspective, conscious action also includes, beyond the elements of consciousness, the essential constitutive characteristics of the act that establish the conditions mandating that an act be *voluntarius*—executed in a manner dictated by will. Therefore conscious action refers to the consciousness of committing an act and includes in a conscious manner the full dynamic and total structure of the act that has been performed. We have to emphasize that throughout this study we will concern ourselves with the conscious act.

In as much as *the act* is concerned, consciousness was implied in the traditional concept of *voluntarium.** The problem facing our study is to furnish an *explication* of consciousness. The Latin term *explicare* clearly indicates that we are moving in the opposite direction from implication.

The need for explication is mandated by the following series of facts: Man acts consciously; man is conscious of his action and who is doing the acting; furthermore, man is also conscious of the act and the self in their dynamic correlation. All of these *consciousnesses* emerge simultaneously, accompanied by conscious action, which at times precede the act, and remain after its completion. Thus consciousness has its own identity and continuity separate from the structure and identity of each separate act. Every act finds an already existing consciousness, passes through it, and leaves a trace behind. Consciousness, on the other hand, mirrors the act when it is born, accompanies it in the process of execution, and, when the act is accomplished, consciousness still reflects it but certainly no longer accompanies it. The accompaniment of the act by consciousness is not so much a proof that acting is conscious, but that man is conscious of his action. And that leads to his acting as a self, which means that the self experiences its action as an act of the self. It is the latter that is the crucial aspect of consciousness and describes its essential role.

The essential function of consciousness is cognition. But this is the most general way of describing its function. Consciousness, properly speaking, is a reflection, or more precisely a mirror, of that which is happening within man and of how man is acting.

In addition, consciousness is also a reflection, or rather a mirror, of everything man comes into contact with. The mediating agent for the contact is some action including cognitive action. Simultaneously, the mirror that is consciousness also encompasses that which is "happening" within man. To repeat, consciousness mirrors all of

* "*Voluntarium*" is the free exercise of will, or the deliberate exercise of an individual's will.—ED.

this at the same instance. It contains the entire man and the entire world accessible to that concrete man (that is, the man who I myself am). How does consciousness contain all this? This important question has to be answered by saying that consciousness contains all of this through means specific to it which could be identified as conscious conscience or consciousness conscious of itself. Thinkers who made consciousness absolute and turned it into the sole subject of all contents (the basis common to all idealistic thinking) did not apparently take under consideration our method of including everything that consciousness does include. In consciousness conscious of itself, its function as an arena for knowledge producing reflection is not performed according to the precise meaning of the word reflect, because consciousness does not have its own subject, is neither a *suppositum* nor an authority from which this function could organically develop.

In order to reach the cognitive acts specific to man, one has to penetrate the object, intellectually objectify it, and thus understand it. For that reason, all cognitive acts have an intentional character; they are clearly directed toward the object of cognition. This intentionality, so characteristic of action, remains alien to consciousness despite its ability to lead to understanding, for example. Consciousness neither penetrates an object nor objectifies it in order to understand it. Consciousness is understanding because its intellectual attribute is beyond doubt and its understanding is an understanding of something that has already been understood within the limits imposed by the degree and method of understanding. Acts of consciousness do not have the characteristic of intentionality, despite the fact that the object of cognition exists in our consciousness as an intellectual picture. However, the intellectual structuring of that image, thus, the entire dynamic side of cognition, is neither the responsibility nor the work of consciousness. Its function is to mirror. This holds true whether we are concerned with isolated acts of consciousness or their totality. The conscious cognitive act is always the same.

It needs to be emphasized, however, that this sum or fraction of the acts of consciousness decides the actual level of consciousness. The subject of that condition is not consciousness but man, whom we correctly describe when we say that he is conscious or not; in full command of his consciousness or only partially so, etc. Consciousness itself does not exist as a "substantive" subject of acts of consciousness. It does not exist as a *suppositum* or an authority.

At this point, it is difficult to justify fully this thesis. This task belongs either to psychology or integral anthropology.

Man does not enter the world of objects only cognitively. He does not even find himself in the world as such an object. He contains his entire world in the mirror that is his consciousness. He lives with this image in his deepest interior, personally and intimately. This results from the ability of consciousness not only to mirror but to internalize in a specific manner that which it mirrors; consciousness creates for it a place in the "I" of the self. We are now, however, touching upon the deeper function of consciousness, which requires a separate discussion.

The reflective function of consciousness is not its sole or complete function. In addition to reflection, consciousness connects with experience. Both are specific to man and both are tremendously important for the understanding of the self in relation to the act and, conversely, of the act in relation to the self. There is more to consciousness than its role as a mirror placed before an act to reflect it in its relationship to the personal "I." Consciousness is not, as it were, a mirror placed there externally. The mirroring function of consciousness leads us with great determination to the interior of acts and to the core of their dynamic relationship with the personal"I"; in this process, the role of consciousness not only changes but completes itself. *Consciousness enables us to have an internal view of our acts and their connection with the personal "I." Consciousness also permits us to experience an act as a personal experience. Due to consciousness, we can fully subjectify that which is objective.* In consciousness, the person and the act are subjectified in their interrelationship (which is a precise correlation). Equally subjectified is everything which constitutes the intentional *world of the self.**

Reflexiveness appears to be the quality most germane to a description of consciousness. This quality is most indicative of the actual level of consciousness and is equally applicable to its separate and total functions within man. The reflexiveness of consciousness indicates its natural turn in the direction of the subject itself. Reflexiveness differs from the reflective capacity specific to the human

* The world structured by the self through its acts.—ED.

mind and its acts. This differentiation is based on the fact that reflexiveness assumes the intentionality of acts of thought, and therefore their concern with objects. Thinking becomes reflexive when we turn our attention to acts previously executed in order to encompass fully their objective content, character or structure. Reflexive thinking is an important element in the creation of all understanding, all knowledge; thus, it is also an important element in the creation of knowledge about the self, which is the same as self-knowledge. This type of thinking serves consciousness directly and contributes to its growth within man.This assertion is quite clear in the light of the aforementioned. Consciousness by itself, however, does not continue this thinking on its own. *Essential for consciousness is the intellectual turn in the direction of the subject itself (as such). Consciousness is reflexive and not reflective.*

This turning of the intellect is an action that is quite different from the reflective function of consciousness. In reflection, the subject is still contained as an object.

The reflexive turn of consciousness causes a subject to experience its own "I." Man is the subject of his existence and action. Man is this subject and also a being endowed with a specific nature, a fact that has its consequences in action.

In his totality, man is given meaning as the direct experience of a being that is the subject of existence and action. Man is given to himself as an "I," and that occurs not only consciously but also in the form of objectification through self-knowledge. I not only have the consciousness of the personal "I," but due to consciousness, I experience that "I," thus I experience myself as a subject. Consciousness is an aspect and more than an aspect—it is a real factor that defines subjectivity in the psychological sense and even more precisely in an experiential sense. To a certain extent, consciousness creates the personal "I."

It is worthwhile to concern ourselves with the road that leads from reflection to experiencing, because that is the road of consciousness. Consciousness is tied to being, that is, to the concrete man who is "myself" and objectively represents some sort of an "I." Consciousness reveals to us *being from the inside* of that concrete human being which is the self. This is the reflexive function of consciousness if we comprehend that function in its entirety.

Due to this function, man exists in complete harmony with his intellectual being while also existing for his interiority. This beingness equates with experience. *Experience in no way determines the sort of reflection that appears on the surface of the being of man or of his action. Just the opposite—experience determines the form in which the being and action that man owes to consciousness are realized.* In a manner of speaking, that form is definitive and final. In it are realized the real and objective energies contained in man, and these are realized in an objective manner and in the profile of his subjectivity. *In his experience, man finds his subjective completion.*

In as far as consciousness is only a reflection, it remains in a quasi-objective distance in relation to the personal "I." If, however, consciousness creates the basis for experience, and if, due to its reflexive capacity, it constitutes that experience, then consciousness eliminates that distance of subject, enters into it, and experientially relates the subject to all other experiences. Quite clearly, consciousness reflects in a different manner than it constitutes: Thanks to self-knowledge, it reflects by retaining its objective meaning. It constitutes in the pure subjectivity of experience. This is very important. Due to this duality of function, which is at the disposal of consciousness, we are able to remain within the sphere of our own subjectivity without losing the feeling of our own being in its real objectification. Our experiences are structured in consciousness; without consciousness, there is no real human experiencing in man [despite the fact that there is a variety of manifestations of life and a variety of actualizations]. *Consciousness confirms and verifies the definition of man,* because it also contains *rationale.* And this indirectly confirms and verifies *human spirituality.* The spirituality of man appears in consciousness and creates in experience the experiential interiority of his being and acting. The basis for the spirituality of man and, in a manner of speaking, its roots lie beyond the immediate reach of experience. We reach them through the process of understanding. Spirituality, however, has its own experiential expression, which is, in a way, a sum of manifestations. The essential relationship between the personal experience of man with the reflexive function of consciousness (which includes intentionality and the act) proves our statement about spirituality. Man can experience himself and all that is within him, his entire world spiritually and intellectually, because consciousness is spiritual and intellectual.

How does man experience his acts? We already know what it means to say that he is conscious of them—and how he understands the conscious reflection of an act. In addition to this, however, man experiences his acts as well as all other acts due to the reflexive function of consciousness. Man experiences his own act as *action*, which is causally connected with the personal "I." Man clearly differentiates this action from all else that "is happening" within his personal "I." In the differentiation between *actio* and *passio*, he finds, within the personal "I," his first experiential base. The differentiation itself is an act of self-knowledge and belongs to the meaning aspect of conscious reflection. This, of course, is paired with experiencing: Man experiences his action as something entirely different from some kind of *action* that occurs within him. Man experiences his morality, moral values, good and evil (or, as it is sometimes popularly and erroneously referred to, his morality and immorality) only in connection with action that is in an act. Again, he is not conscious of the morality of his acts but authentically experiences the morality. *The act, morality, and moral values not only function objectively in the sense in which consciousness reflects them, but they also function simultaneously through subjectivity for which this consciousness bears direct responsibility.* Because consciousness always turns to the subject as a subject, it causes the experiencing of the subjectivity of every act and of its moral value.

2

The Individual and the Common Good: Toward a Theory of Participation

God's essence is no more "lord" of the world
than man is "lord and king" of creation;
but both are, above all,
companions of each other's fate,
enduring, overcoming, some day perhaps
victorious.

MAX SCHELER

THE next rung on the ladder leading toward maturity and substance is attained when a person, acting consciously, moves beyond himself and the inner circle of family, friends, and acquaintances into the physical world of experience.

To help overcome alienation and break down the barriers separating a person from his fellows, John Paul II argues that it is necessary to develop an ethical system that allows him to unfold in consciousness and freedom.

On this level, man acts as a whole person able to give, to receive, and to share his humanity with others. And as such, he fosters the growth of awareness within his community, becomes a model for others, contributes to the common good, and comes to realize that the share he contributes is part of the grand design that helps him become what he was meant to be.

Once again, the selections are taken from The Controversy about Man *and* The Self and the Act.

From *The Controversy about Man*

Interaction

As we remarked in the introduction, our analysis is concerned with the relationship between the subjectivity of man as an individual and the structure of the human community. . . . A community does not take shape merely because several people live and act together or because one person interacts with others. Community doesn't simply denote an aggregation of individuals, but a specific entity that serves to unify that aggregation. . . . Any investigation of the frame of reference applying to a given aggregation cannot simply posit an objective reality that affects every member of such a social unit equally, but must make a point of focusing on the consciousness and personal experience of the members, as it were, individually. Only by taking this approach, do we perceive the reality of a community and begin to grasp its essential meaning. . . .

Relationships

At this point, we must concern ourselves with the problem of the relationship between society's values and man's own sense of purpose. There is no real reason to doubt the fact that man living in society attains self-realization in community with others and, beyond that, with the help of society itself. But even if this is so, can self-fulfillment and self-realization be understood as a mere function of society, and can the individual's own goals be subordinated to the expediencies of society (or even a collective of societies)? To provide an answer to this question, we must consider two more, apparently unrelated, aspects or dimensions of human society. First, we shall deal with that sphere of interpersonal relations symbolized by the "I-Thou" formula and, second, by the "We" formula, descriptive of social rather than interpersonal relationships. . . .

As I conceptualize or utter the word "thou," I am aware that the particular human being I am addressing in this fashion is one of many who could be thus addressed; that I do address (and experience) a number of other persons at other times and places in this fashion and that I might indeed address any person whatever in this way. To be sure, the potential exists for my extending the "I-Thou" relationship to all of mankind; but reality, in effect, restricts the relationship to myself and one other. . . .

I and Thou

Let us assume that the "I-Thou" relationship runs full cycle and reverts to the person who initiated it—then this very return flow becomes the agent serving to actualize the original "I" on the basis of its relation with a "Thou." It appears, however, that this process alone does not suffice to create community; but it is important for a more complete experience of self on the part of the "I," a cognition of its own self "in the light of a second 'I'." . . . It is an indication of the actual nature of this type of community that human beings are revealed to each other as personal subjects. But, there is a didactic dimension inherent in this structure as well: Any interpersonal relationship should reach fulfillment in a mutual revelatory experience, in man experiencing his fellow man's personal subjectivity in all its facets.

In any "I-Thou" relationship, men should be revealed to each other in the original essence of their being—in self-possession and self-disposition and, above all, in their urge toward self-realization, which manifests itself to the highest degree in man's conscience, thereby revealing his immanent transcendence as an individual. Men should not only be revealed to each other in this truth of their personal reality; they should be accepted and confirmed in it as well. Such acceptance and affirmation is the moral bedrock upon which interpersonal community is founded.

The Social Dimension

"We" signifies several people, several or many individuals, who coexist and are involved in common actions of some sort. . . . "Common," in this instance, indicates that these actions and the existence of these many selves along with them are tied to some value that therefore deserves to be called the common good. . . . The relationship of these selves to the common good appears to constitute the nucleus of the social community. . . . Let us take marriage as an example. The "I-Thou" relationship, which is the determinant of marriage, assumes a social dimension as soon as husband and wife subscribe to those values that can be characterized as the common good of marriage and—at least potentially—of the family. Their relation to this good makes their community of being and action appear in a different light: It becomes a "We" relationship and a social dimension of two human beings (rather than one plus one) who nonetheless continue to be an "I" and a "Thou" for each other. . . .

COMMONWEAL

The commonweal essentially denotes what is good for many and, by implication, for all. In fact, the numbers tend to vary: In a marriage, two people are involved; in a family, several; in individual nations, millions; and in all of mankind, billions. And because the good is defined differently in each instance, the concept of the commonweal is best expressed in terms of analogy (in the analogy of proportionality). What constitutes the commonweal in marriage or in the family is not synonymous with what constitutes the commonweal in a nation, nor in mankind as a whole. In fact, each society or social group in which the human "We" is actualized will arrive at its own particular definition of the commonweal. . . . In the final analysis, the superior worth of the common good is based on the fact that the good of each individual member of the We-community gains fuller expression in the common good and attains a higher degree of fulfillment in it. Thus, with the help of the common good, the individual experiences himself more profoundly and more extensively in the human "We." . . . We Poles know from historical experience what a high price individual citizens have paid time and again for the good that bears the name of "Poland" or "our country." The sacrifices that have been made for the realization of this good, the offering-up of the goods of countless individuals—involving deportation, imprisonment, and death—bore witness and bear witness still to the magnitude of this good and its overriding importance. . . . The superiority of the common good, which corresponds to the transcendence of the individual, is experienced and accepted by conscience; if it is not, conflicts tend to arise. This is why research in the field of social ethics focuses on the question of the common good. The history of the nations of the world and the development of the different social systems have both shown that—despite all the efforts to attain the "true" common good, which might subsume the nature of the social "We" and the personal transcendence of the self—a wide variety of utilitarianisms, totalitarian systems, as well as forms of social egotism have arisen. . . .

"We" stands for more than just a multitude of individuals; it not only points to many human selves, but to the peculiar subjectivity of this plural mode or, at least, to the determined effort to attain such subjectivity. These efforts differ widely, of course, both as to perception and execution, depending on the various "We's" and the peculiarities of a specific community: be it a marriage or a family, a particular environment, a people, a state, or mankind as a whole. . . . The human selves in these various spheres are prepared not only to look out for themselves, but also to help realize what is essential for the "We" of the social community. In other words, they stand ready to help realize the subjectivity of many or, for that matter, all human beings on the basis of this community and in conformity with their own human nature. . . . Social community is never simply conferred upon man as a gift, but proposed to him as a task to be fulfilled. All this proves the thesis of the priority of the personal subject vis-à-vis the community. Unless this priority is preserved, the concept of the individual as an end-in-itself is annihilated, and man's unimpeded movement toward meaning as such is thwarted. . . .

Participation and Alienation

As a result of our discussion thus far, the nature of participation and its opposite, alienation, should now be clear. . . . The "I-Thou" relationship creates a direct, open channel from one person to another. In this case participation means turning toward another self on the basis of personal transcendence, toward the fullness of truth of this other person, toward humanity, one might say. . . . Alienation is the opposite of participation, its antithesis. As is well known, the concept of alienation plays an important role in Marxist philosophy. But apart from that, it has its proper place in contemporary human thought as one aspect of modern anthropology. . . . We believe that alienation is an essentially individual problem and as such, of course, a humanistic and ethical question. Alienation . . .

causes man to lose his capacity for self-realization within the community to some extent—both in the "We" and in the "I-Thou" sphere. . . . Social alienation means that the sum total of individuals, each of whom is a specific "I," is unable to develop unmolested toward the authentic "We." The social process, which is meant to lead to genuine subjectivity for all, is impeded or even thwarted because man cannot assume his identity as an individual within its confines. Social life takes place outside and beyond him; it does not really turn against him, but goes on, as it were, "at his expense." He may be living and acting "in communion with others," but does not attain self-realization in the process. Whether the We-community is merely limited in its scope or actually annihilated will depend on the extent of alienation not only as it applies to one individual or another, but, beyond that, to entire groups of a society, to classes, or even to whole peoples. . . .

Analogously . . . this trend has also emerged in the interpersonal sphere, in the "I-Thou" relationship. It cannot be quantitatively compared; but qualitatively, the experience may often be much more poignant because human relations would seem to concentrate on the "I-Thou" rather than the "We" sphere. In this context, alienation as the obverse of participation signifies a limitation or annihilation of all the values by which one man can know another as a second "I." Under such circumstances, it is extremely difficult to experience true humanity, i.e., the essential personal values of the individual encountered as "Thou." The "I" never enters into the equation; it fails to make the connection and is therefore unable to find its own self. Interpersonal relations no longer include one's "neighbor." We are left with the "other," the stranger, and, at length, with the enemy. . . . Community is thereby disfigured, wasting away along with the experience of humanity, which draws people close and binds them together. . . . Negating and standing in opposition to participation, alienation does not rob man of his birthright as an individual member of the species, but it does place the personal self in peril. Participation, however, in antithesis to alienation, confirms the self and permits the individual to unfold. In this sense, we may speak of participation as a specific determinant of the individual because it helps him attain self-realization both in interpersonal and social relationships.

From *The Self and the Act*

Towards a Theory of Participation

The point of departure for these reflections was the conviction that an act is a specific revelation of the self. The same road that led to the recognition of the self will also lead to a deeper understanding of the act. The act not only serves as a means or a unique base from which to view the self, but also reveals its dimensions to the self. The entire *road of cognition* that we have so far traversed has led to an understanding of an exact *correlation* of the self and the act, a correlation in which the person and the act emerged as two elements—as two polarities in constant interaction. They serve to reveal each other and are explanatory one in terms of the other. The basic line of interpretation of the self and the act emerges by degrees from this correspondence and correlation.

The concern of this chapter is the dynamic correlation of the self and the act *which is* a function of the fact that acts are committed by people "jointly with others."

The expression "jointly with" is neither sufficient nor precise enough; at this moment, however, it seems to be the most appropriate if we desire to emphasize the variety of relations that has the quality of jointness or sociability—a quality most frequently associated with human acts. This is the simple and natural consequence of the fact that man lives "jointly with others"; it could even be said that he exists together with others. The feature of this togetherness or sociability is imprinted on human existence.

This fundamental fact, as well as its consequences in the field of action, bring us closer to the understanding of that reality which we usually describe as *society.* In this chapter, we do not, however, intend to concern ourselves with society; we do not even want to begin with the assertion that human acts have a social character. We refuse to do this because such reflections would lead us to a different level that would—from the point of view of content and methodology—be essentially different from the dimension in which we have been moving and within which we intend to remain. We shall persist until the very end of this book to concern ourselves with the self and the act.

In this, the last chapter, we wish to render more explicit the aspect of the dynamic correlation of the self and the act that stems from the fact of existing and acting "jointly with others." This fact could also be identified as cooperative action, although there is a visible difference between these expressions. "To act jointly with others" means something different from "to cooperate." Therefore, at the beginning at least, we shall consistently use the expression "jointly with others." This expression is sufficiently ambiguous to enable us to make differentiations and conduct the analysis that would make the term more precise, which, in the context of our study, will be necessary.

It is known that human acts are performed in a setting involving a variety of intra-human and social relations. By using the formulation, acting "jointly with others," we include all of these possible relations without specifically concerning ourselves with any one of them. All of these relations, regardless of their form, are an aspect of the act and also form the dynamic *correlation* of the self and the act. So far we have not sufficiently emphasized this aspect. This aspect is simply the consequence of the *internal logic of the study, which leads to the conclusion that the only possible way truly to understand action is through a correct interpretation of cooperation* and not the other way around. The dynamism of the correlation of the act with the self is in itself the fundamental reality and retains this quality regardless of the type of action undertaken, "jointly with others." It is only on the grounds of this fundamental correlation that any act "jointly with others" can acquire its specific human meaning. This is the basic sequence that can neither be ignored nor neglected.

It is, however, quite evident that the fact of acting "jointly with others" in a variety of relationships and dependencies creates new problems. The field of sociology alone indicates the tremendous range of subjects identified as society and social existence, and by inference concerns itself with man as member of a variety of societies and communities, and with his sociability, all of which affect his actions. In this study, however, *we do not intend to undertake the problem of acting in its sociological range, and we will especially avoid its sociological specificity.* That, too, would involve moving the study to another level. This study will remain deliberately and consistently on the level of the self and the act. We are so directed by the conviction that the dynamic correlation of the act with the self is the fundamental reality underlying all actions of a social, communal, or intra-personal character. Acts committed by a man as a member of diverse societies, social groupings, or communities remain acts of a self. The social or communal aspects of these acts have their roots in the self and not the other way around. It is, however, indispensable for the explanation of the personal character of human acts to understand the consequences of the fact that these acts occur "jointly with others." How does this fact make itself evident in the dynamic correlation of the act with the self? The answer to this question is especially important because acting "jointly with others" is such a common occurrence. This answer will emerge through the reflections that follow.

We used the word "participation" in the title of this chapter to emphasize the problem we wish to deal with; we also used it because it indicates the resolution of the problem. This contention is based on a conviction that the element of participation parallels the dynamic correlation of the act with the self. Participation renders explicit the reality of acting "jointly with others." Participation as an element, however, requires thorough explanation.

The Personalistic Value of the Act

In order to give this explanation we have to glance quickly over the main elements of the analysis given in the preceding chapters which revealed to us the extremely personalistic content of the act. This analysis also indicates that *the mere performance of an act by a self determines its fundamental value.* It could be identified as the "personalistic" or personal value of the act. This value differs from all other moral values, which are evaluated in relation to a norm, while the personalistic value is entirely contained within the performance of an act by a self. It is contained within the fact that "man acts" in a manner specific to himself. Consequently, the kind of acting is an authentic self-determination. In the performance of an act occurs a transcending of the self that has consequences of a somatic and psychic nature. The personalistic value, which is essentially contained in the fact of a person's accomplishing an act, includes *within itself an entire series of values* associated either with the (profile) process of transcendence or integration. Although both of them contribute to the performance of an act, they still retain a separateness as values. For example, the synthesis of an act with a motion adds some sort of a value that differs from the value resulting from a synthesis of an act with emotion, yet both may be included in the dynamic totality of performing an act. Each value, in its own way, conditions and fulfills self-determination.

The *personalistic* value of a human act is a unique expression of the persons themselves. In this study we will not be fundamentally concerned with the axiology (value structure) of a person. Rather, we are engaged in a study of a person's ontology. It would appear, however, that this approach would yield a fuller knowledge of the axiology of a person. This is equally true as far as the value of a person itself is concerned, and illuminates the knowledge of a variety of values as well as the establishment of their actual hierarchy. In spite of the dictum *operari sequitur esse* (acting follows being), according to which the self and its value is prior and basic to the value of the act, the self reveals itself through an act. We have maintained the correctness of this proposition since the very beginning of the book. Therefore, the *personalistic* value of an act stands in the closest possible relationship to the performance of an act by a self. It yields a specific source and basis for the recognition of the value of the person, as well as of the other values and their hierarchy contained within that person. This essential *correlation* of the act with the self is equally applicable to the axiology and ontology of the self.

The personalistic value of an act is hereby *fundamentally differentiated from strictly moral values of an accomplished act that are established by a reference to a norm.* The difference is evident because the *personalistic* value of the act precedes and conditions its moral values. It is quite clear that any kind of moral value, like good or evil, presumes that the act has already been fully performed. If an act has not been fully executed, if it shows incompleteness in the sphere of authentic self-determination, then the moral value loses its basis to a certain degree. The expression of any judgment of moral values ascribed to a human being . . . has to begin with the establishment of causality, responsibility, and self-determination. In other words, *we have to make certain that a given human person has actually performed an act.* This is precisely the subject of many traditional works concerning the *voluntarium.* These studies involved enormous research and caused many disputes, and both the research and the disputes have been very penetrating.

We do not regard the performance of an act by a person solely in its ontological meaning. *The performance of an act by a person is in itself a value.* This is precisely the *personalistic* value that means that a person performing an act performs in it his own self. . . . The fulfillment of the self in an act is closely related to an ethical value because *nonfulfillment* of a self in the performance of an act is a moral evil. However, this close relationship between ethical and personalistic values is not the same as an identity of the two. The personalistic value consists of the fact that in an act a person actualizes himself, a process through which expression is given to the specific structure of self-possession and self-supremacy. The ethical value has its roots in this actualization, which we describe here as fulfillment. The ethical value emerges from the personalistic value, penetrates it, but does not identify with it.

. . . In thinking about human action, it is the personalistic value that enables us to determine if an act fully measures up to standards or if it contains flaws in its performance. A certain thought suggests itself in comparing this study to the traditional method of conceptualization in which human acts (*actibus humanis*) were differentiated on the basis of *voluntarium perfectum* and *voluntarium imperfectum.* The term *voluntarium* indicates the will as the authority on which the performance of the act depends. This means in this study that the performance of the act, the fulfillment, and the self are fused into one without implying the rejection of the traditional approach, but suggesting a way of completing the traditional by thinking it through to its conclusion. Will as authority is contained within the self. The will is within its self-determination through which the self reveals its own structure. This is why we suggest that the reduction of *voluntarium* to mere will as authority might cause an impoverishment of the reality that an act is.

Moreover, the revealing of the dynamic correlation of the act with the self, as well as the attempt to explain it, will lead us directly and immediately to the personalistic value of the act. The analysis of human action conducted on the level of authority seems to limit the meaning of an act to ontology on the basis of which emerges only an *ethical* axiology, that is, moral values that result from the relationship of an act to an ethical norm. Sometimes it even appears that an act has only meaning as an instrument of the entire ethical order. The personalistic value of the act, which we have been attempting to sketch throughout this study, convinces us of the authenticity of the personalistic value, which, in the strictest sense, is not yet an ethical one; but nonetheless it endows the human act with its proper fullness. The fullness flows from the dynamic depth of the self, which, in turn, enables us to understand better the ethical values in their closest possible relevance to the self and the entire world of "selves."

All of this is of extreme importance to the subject of this chapter, "that man acts jointly with others." What are the consequences of the dynamic correlations of an act with the self? We asked this question previously. Now we shall raise a second question, which further defines the first one: What is the relationship of acting "jointly with others" to the personalistic value of the act?

By phrasing the question in this manner, we imply a whole series of questions, but fundamentally what we wish to find out is how a man acting "jointly with others" in a whole variety of inter-human relations manages to fulfill and realize himself. How, under these conditions, does an act retain this fusion with the self, which we described as being both a transcendence of the self and an integration of the self in the act? How, in the process of acting "jointly with others," do acts maintain that hierarchy of values that result equally from the process of transcending and integration?

By raising the question of means in the way we did, the very tone of the question seems to indicate an absence of any doubt that we are asking the question relevant to acting "jointly with others" in a manner that opens up the entire problem. If there is a doubt, it is a *methodological one.* This doubt clearly permeates contemporary thought and philosophy. *Perhaps it is connected in human philosophy to the position of the self.* Traditional human philosophy—even when concerned with the self—was clearly anchored "in the grounds of nature." According to it, man is an element of rational nature and as such is a self. Simultaneously, his nature is *social.* In relationship to these concepts, thinking about man advances not so much in the direction of some sort of fundamental questioning of this philosophy as it proceeds in a search for a more adequate explanation and a more detailed picture. No one doubts that man is an element of rational nature; neither is there any doubt that he has a *social nature.* However, we are asking: What does all of this mean? In the context of our study, what is the meaning of these assertions in the perspective of the dynamic correlation of the act with the self? Our question leads toward an explanation of what is contained in the assertion that man has a social nature. We are concerned with elaborating, extending, perfecting our view of the self. At the same time, we are returning to the point of departure for our enterprise, which led to the confirmation that the social nature of man could be nothing else but the very experience that man exists and acts "jointly with others"—an event that occurs in some way accidentally to every human being.

The questions we raised about this occurrence are not of secondary but primary importance. They do not question the social character of human nature but tend to explain it on the level of the self while also taking under consideration the entire dynamic picture that emerged from the previous analysis. At this point, in order to answer our questions, and as a key to these answers we have to describe more precisely the meaning of the concept *participation.* This concept has been previously mentioned in relation to "acting jointly with others." *Participation* has a general and a philosophical meaning. The common meaning of this term is "to take part in." We say that someone participated in a meeting—this means that he took part in a meeting. We are stating a simple fact in a most general way. It is practically a statistical observation, without attempting to discover the basis of this participation. *The philosophical meaning of participation, however, mandates that we search for this basis.* In its philosophical meaning, the term *participation* has an old and very rich history in the language of philosophy and theology. Obviously, in this study, we are concerned with the philosophical meaning. We are not concerned with the affirmation of the fact that participation by a concrete man is some action "jointly with others," but we are concerned with revealing the basis—the reasons—for this participation.

We have to reach the basics *that are contained within the self.* (This search will be different; it will lead to different conclusions for the application of the term *participation* than those usually derived on the basis of traditional philosophy, which finds the meaning of this concept a derivative of nature.)

By the term *participation,* we understand an event that occurs on the basis of a correspondence to the transcendence of the self in the act when this act is performed "jointly with others." Obviously, if this act corresponds to transcendence, it also corresponds to integration because both are in a complimentary relationship to each other. *This characteristic of participation indicates, therefore, that man acting "jointly with others" maintains in that action the personalistic value of his own act and at the same time helps implement that which is contemplated by the cooperative aspect of the action.* This statement can be turned around by saying that due to participation man acting "jointly with others" *keeps all that which results from cooperative action and because of it simultaneously concretizes the personalistic value of his own act.*

In this second formulation it is very important to emphasize the expression "because of it." This expression indicates the proper character of *participation.* To begin with, it makes clear that the concept *participation* is applied here for the purpose of reaching the very foundations for acting "jointly with others." These foundations are contained within the self and are germane to it.

Yet, it is also clear that everything that determines the personalistic value of the act—its performance, transcendence, and integration—are not only preserved due to this participation but are also made real—rendered concrete.

Participation, therefore, means that the self has an internal homogenous quality that confirms that while acting "jointly with others" it does so because the self acts as a self. In as far as acting itself is concerned—acting "jointly with others" brings out the quality of the person which confirms that in such an act the self fulfills itself. Participation thus determines the personalistic value of every form of cooperation or, more specifically, of acting "jointly with others." Since this gives rise to a variety of limitations of self-determination, it creates the necessity of transcending the self and integrating its action with those of the others. Truly, the limiting of the personalistic value at times goes so far that it becomes difficult even to talk about acting "jointly with others," in the sense of an authentic act of a self. Under certain circumstances, action can be transformed into a passive form of action that occurs in a person under the influence of others. An extreme example of this is action under the impact of what is called mass psychology—or action of a most uncontrollable character.

We have all of this in mind while reflecting on the correct meaning of the concept *participation.* Participation in a variety of relations to action "jointly with others" presents itself as a form of accommodation to these relations. Yet the term *relation* also implies a differentiated attitude in the relationship maintained with "others."

In order to create at least a general analytical frame for an explanation of these attitudes and of the content of participation, we have to continue in our attempt to understand the objective and subjective meanings of the phrase "acting jointly with others.". . . Participation not only denotes a variety of forms of relationship with others (individual and society), but also includes the foundations for these relationships, which are contained within the self and are responsible to the self. Participation corresponds to the transcendence and integration of the self in the act. Simultaneously, a human being, acting "jointly with others," realizes his authentic personalistic value. This means that the human being performs an act, and in its performance, performs his self. The transcendence and integration of the self occurs in the act performed "jointly with others" even if that performance is the consequence of a decision to perform it made by others. The self perceives in the object of the act a value that in some sense is its own, and homogeneous. Closely related to all of this is the sense of self-determination. Self-determination in the instance of acting "jointly with others" contains and expresses participation.

When we assert that participation is a quality of the self, we refer to a concrete being in a dynamic correlation with the act. The use of the term correlation conveys the meaning of participation in an act which renders concrete the objectives of a commonality [group]. Moreover the objective of the action "jointly with others" in which the individual actor participated concretizes also the personalistic value of his own act. The actualization—the implementation of a program—results from the potential to realize it.

Individualism and Anti-individualism

The concept of *participation* that we are now developing has a theoretical meaning. It is an attempt to explain participation on the grounds of the dynamic correlation of the act with the self—meaning the correlation with that which is in reality the social nature of man. This form of conceptualization is simultaneously theoretical and empirical in the sense that the theory of participation explains the experiential fact of actions and existence "jointly with others." We must, however, perceive at the same time that the *theory has indirectly a normative meaning.* It indicates not only how a self acting "jointly with others" realizes in this action its own self, but also indirectly indicates a certain obligation imposed on the self that comes as a consequence of the principle of participation. There exists a mutuality in participation: On the one hand, by participating, a self releases the personalistic value of its act, and on the other hand, all participatory types of activity should be structured in such a way that the self, which is included in that form of action, is given the opportunity to realize (concretize) its own self.

This is the normative content that has so far emerged from our analysis of participation. The normative and theoretical meaning of participation penetrates a variety of structures subsumed under the phrase of "acting jointly with others." It also penetrates the personalistic value to which participation directly corresponds and on which it is based. If the personalistic value is the fundamental value . . . ethical values and the ethical value structure . . . also have a fundamental meaning. The norm we suggest is not, in the strictest sense of the word, ethical (meaning a norm of an act based on its objective content). The norm we refer to is the norm contained in the performance of the act itself . . . ; it is an "internal" norm that is concerned with the self-determining quality of the self. Self-determination implies causality as well as transcendence and integration in the performance of the act. We have sufficiently emphasized this subject so that the delineation between a strictly ethical value structure and a personalistic one has been sufficiently clearly established.

However, the personalistic value conditions the ethical value structure through action and participation in such a way that it determines the ethical. An act has to be performed not only in order to have an ethical value that can be ascribed to it—but in order to enable a self to have the basic and *natural* (stemming from the fact that it is a self) right to perform acts and to fulfill itself in these acts. This right receives the real meaning of a "right" on the basis of acting "jointly with others." It is at this point that the normative meaning of participation is confirmed. However, the ground of "acting jointly with others" in *the performance of acts which at the same time are the fulfillment of the self in those acts,* on which depends the acts' personalistic value, is precisely the same ground on which the personalistic value of these acts can be annihilated. The first way in which this can happen is if the participation is not the consequence of a determination by the self to participate in the actions. The second way that this can occur is by preventing participation through reasons that originate outside of the self and are the consequence of the way in which the joint action is structured.

At this point in our analysis, we are touching upon the implications inherent in two systems: one that is identified as *individualism* and the other one, which has many names in our times, from among which we have chosen *objective totalism.* In simpler terms, this system could be identified as anti-individualism. We are not contemplating analysis of these systems, but are restricting ourselves to their implications.... These systems have an axiological (value-structured) meaning and, indirectly, an ethical one: Individualism posits the good of the individual as the supreme good, which demands that the good of the society and community should be subjected to it. Objective totalism posits the diametrically opposed principle in which the individual is unconditionally subject to the good of the community and society. It is evident that each of these systems sees the supreme good and forms the basis for norms in opposites.... However, we intend to touch upon these systems only to the extent that they have a bearing on our concern with the self and the act in all of the varieties contained in the phrase "acting jointly with others."

In "acting jointly with others," we discover the principle of participation as an essential characteristic and at the same time as a particular source of law and duty. This is the law of performing acts that serve the self and at the same time are cognizant of the fact that this performance contains a personalistic value. The two orientations enumerated above limit participation from opposite directions....

Individualism accomplishes this by isolating the self ... to itself and to its own good, that is, a good that exists in isolation from the good of the others and from the common good. In this system, the good of the individual has the quality of being opposed to every other individual and his good. This kind of individualism is based on self-preservation and is always on the defensive, and is also defective. Acting and existing jointly with others is, according to this individualism, an imposed necessity to which an individual has to submit. But there is no positive aspect in this necessity. It does not serve the development of his individuality. "The others" are for the individual only a source of limitations and may even be opponents and create polarization. . . . *The implications of this position is contradictory to the meaning of participation we gave this concept previously.* This position does not have the quality that would enable a self to fulfill itself by acting "jointly with others."

The negation of participation is also the characteristic of the system we identified as *objective totalism.* . . . Its dominant characteristic is the necessity to protect itself from individuality, which is perceived basically as an enemy of the community and of the common good. This is the consequence of the assumption that an individual exists only for his own good and has no disposition to fulfill himself through acting and existing jointly with others. Since there is no quality of participation, the common good can be created only through the limitation of the individual. The common good has a total preeminence. This good can not be independently selected on the basis of participation—it is imposed on the individual and limits him. Under such circumstances, the fulfillment of the common good can only occur as a function of coercion. This presentation is again a quick overview of the thought process characteristic of anti-individualism. . . . Both the *individualistic system* and the *anti-individualistic system* reveal *the same method of thinking about man.*

. . . The hallmark of the personalistic method of thinking about man is the conviction that the potential to participate is a part of the self. It is obvious that this potential has to be activated, formed, and cultivated in order to bring it to its fullest realization. . . . Man lives and acts with others not only because it is his *nature* to do so, but also because in this acting and being "jointly with others" he can reach his level of maturity, . . . the level of maturity of the self. For this reason one has to recognize everyone's *fundamental right to act and thus everyone's freedom to act,* through the exercise of which the self fulfills itself. The meaning of this right as well as of this freedom is contained in the personalistic value of the human act. On the basis of this value and because of this value, man has the right to complete freedom of action. Individualism and anti-individualism have to be utterly excluded because of their faulty interpretations and lack of understanding of the personalistic value of an act. . . . A self finds fulfillment only in a moral good; evil is always some sort of nonfulfillment. The thing is clear: Man has the freedom of action, the right to act, but does not have the right to do wrong. This determinism stems from law and corresponds simultaneously to the personalistic value structure.

Participation and Communal Membership

As we have previously noted, individualism and totalism germinate in the same soil. Their common root is the conception of man as an entity more or less bereft of the capacity to participate. This way of thinking is reflected in the concept of *living-in-society,* in the axiology of society and the social ethics that evolve from this assumption. We are not concerned in this study with tracing the varieties of individualisms and anti-individualisms. . . . It is only necessary to state that on the basis of this way of thinking about man, which is so characteristic of both systems, we can not find an authentic basis for a human community. The concept *community* expresses the reality that we have emphasized throughout this chapter when we have referred to being and acting "jointly with others." *However, community remains clearly tied to the experience of the self that we have tried to trace from . . . the start of this chapter.* We are discovering the reality of participation as the quality of the self that acts "jointly with others" basically because it finds its own fulfillment in this form of action. Participation as a quality of the self creates its own *constitutivum* of community. Due to this quality, the self and the community are, in a way, contiguous and are neither strange nor opposite to each other. These qualities appear only in the individualistic and anti-individualistic methods of thinking about man.

In order to explain even more fully the meaning of participation, let us now look at it from the point of view of the community. As a matter of fact, we have been doing this from the start by using the expression "jointly with others." . . . The concept *community* corresponds to this expression, but we introduced . . . into it a new *objectivity.* While we were talking about being and acting "jointly with others," we clearly saw the human self as the subject of this form of being and acting. When we begin to consider *community,* we can replace the adverbial form "acting jointly with others" by the use of the (grammatical) *subject* form and an abstraction. This new subjectivity is the contribution of a . . . collectivity or, generally speaking, a group. It is an *as if subjectivity because the substantive object of being and acting together when it is realized jointly with others is always the man-self.* The expressions *commune, sociability,* or *society* indicate a random order. Being and acting jointly does not create a new subject for action; it only introduces new relationships between people who are the real acting subjects. It is absolutely necessary to express this reservation on the margin of all reflections concerning communities.

It seems that this concept (community) even in its grammatical form as subject and its abstract meaning is especially close to the dynamic reality of self and participation. . . . We are on the same level of reflection and research that we have maintained from the very beginning of this book, which means that we shall analyze the relationship between participation and membership in a community in the same way we analyzed the relationship between the self and the act. Man in his characteristic dynamism reveals himself within the confines of a community as its member.

There are a variety of expressions that describe this membership in a variety of communities. For example, the expression *relative* states that a person is a member of a family community. The expression *countryman* indicates membership in a national community. The expression *citizen* indicates that a person belongs to a collectivity identified as a *state.* The expression *believer* indicates that a person is a member of a religious community, etc. Every one of these expressions indicates the social affiliation of a person. . . . Since in our study we are searching for the basis of participation, we shall concentrate our efforts *not so much on membership in a society as on membership in a community.* The previously indicated examples of different types of communities indicate that there are many more examples of varieties of communities that crop up in common usage. They describe not only the membership in the community but also the nature of the ties to the community. . . . For example, the expression *brother* or *sister* denotes a much stronger tie to the family community than *relative* does. . . . But there are also expressions that accentuate the commonality of action at the expense of the community in which the action takes place. An example of this is *assistant* or *foreman* or *helper.* In each of these expressions, the linkage is explicit, while the existence of a community is only implied.

All of these expressions imply that a human being is a member of a variety of communities that exist because a human being either lives in them or acts with them. In this study we are even more interested in the commonality of action because we are primarily concerned with the dynamic correlation between the act and the self as the basic source of knowledge. Yet some sort of being together conditions the commonality of action—and this is why we cannot view them entirely separately.

The essential problem, however, is the fact that membership in these communities is not the same as participation. We will illustrate this point by an example. In a group of workers digging the same hole, or in a group of students listening to the same lecture, the fact that there is a commonality of action is certainly evident. Every one of these workers or students is a member of a specific community of action. This community can be perceived in the perspective of the goal of the activity. In the first instance, it is the completion of digging the hole, which might serve later as the foundation of a building. In the second instance, the goal is to become familiar with the subject of the lecture, which, in turn, relates to the totality of a theme and the sum total of these studies to an expertise in a discipline. It can be said that in both instances the participants work to reach the same goal—the completion of their task. This objective unity of reaching the goal helps objectify the commonality of action. *In the objective sense, the commonality of action can be described according to the goal of the action,* which makes people work together. Each one of them is a member of this objective community.

However, in the perspective of the self and the act, not only the objective community is important, *but also its subjective aspect, which we will identify here as participation.* Here we raise the question: Is the human being a member of a commonality of action . . . because these actions fulfill a real act and fulfill the self in these acts? This is what defines participation. Yet, by simply acting "jointly with others," a human being might still remain outside of this community of participation. Thus we are now confronted by a problem that cannot be solved without an examination of the so-called common good. It is known that there are instances of participation based on election: A human being elects that which others elect or even because the others elect. At the same time, he elects because it is for his own good and represents a goal of his own efforts. . . . Participation enables a human being to make such elections or selections and simultaneously enables him to act jointly with others. *Perhaps only under such circumstances can this kind of action be called cooperation.* The mere fact of acting jointly with others however must not yet be classified as cooperation that leads to participation. It is quite possible that on the grounds of action and of being there exists an objective community, but it has no subjective existence (a community of objects without subjects).

Participation and the Common Good

The resolution of the problems of community and participation lies *in the meaning we ascribe to the concept* common good. If we understand common good as meaning the good of the community, we are partially correct—partially, because this meaning may contain a serious one-sidedness. It is the axiological one-sidedness of . . . individualism or anti-individualism.

The objective community of action is easily discernible on the basis of the fact that people act together. . . . This community can very easily be equated with the goal for which this community is working, and this goal can become the common good. . . . However, the equating of the common good with the goal of the activities performed together by people . . . is too hasty and superficial. . . . It can be stated that the *goal* of common action *understood clearly, objectively, and soberly has something of the common good in it,* but does not constitute that common good in its entirety.

. . . The common good can not be described without taking under consideration . . . the subjective aspect, i.e., that aspect of action that stands in relation to the self acting. If we consider this aspect, it has to be stated that the common good is not only the goal achieved by some sort of common action, but, that the primary consideration has to be *under what conditions and in what way does the common action liberate participation within the self that acts jointly, and creates in itself the subjective community of action.* If the common good is understood as a goal, then it must be understood in its objective and subjective meanings. The subjective good is very closely related to participation as an attribute of the self and the act. Seen in this perspective, we can maintain that the common good corresponds to the social nature of man.

. . . We are analyzing the common good as a principle of correct participation due to which a self acting together with others can perform authentic acts and because of which is able to fulfill itself. We are concerned with a truly personalistic structure of human existence in a community—in every community to which a human being may belong. Common good is a good of the community precisely because in the axiological sense it creates the conditions for communal existence—and action stems from that fact. It could be said that *the common good determines through the axiological order the community*, or . . . the society. Acting . . . is considered jointly with . . . existing. However, the common good leads emphatically into the region of existing "jointly with others."

Yet participation in groups whose cohesiveness is based on an obvious community of action is . . . not as strong as is participation in a community based on existence itself—a family, a nation, a religious order. The axiology of such communities, which expresses itself in a common good, is much deeper: . . . The basis for participation is much more demanding, so also is the urge to participate. Every human being expects from these communities of existence that he will be able to select that which others select as their good because his selection of the "common" good will serve the fulfillment of his own self. (These communities of existence have earned the label of *natural societies* because they basically correspond to the social nature of man.) . . . Basing himself on his capacity to participate, which is the basis for existing and being together with others, a human being expects that in communities based on the common good his own actions will serve the community, support it, and enrich it. Within such an axiological structure, a human being is ever ready to give up a variety of personal goods, sacrificing them for the community. This process of sacrificing goes "against nature," but it corresponds to every human being's capacity to participate . . . , and that capacity opens the way to self-fulfillment.

. . . Neither the number nor the generality in the sense of quantity determines the correct character of the common good, but the basis from which it is derived. This method of viewing the common good is a continuation of the critique on individuality and anti-individuality. . . . We perceive with increasing clarity participation as a quality of the self and the act forming the authentic basis for a human community.

ANALYSIS OF ATTITUDES: AUTHENTIC ATTITUDES

On the basis of reflections of the real meaning of the common good . . . of the relationship that occurs between participation as a quality of the self and the good of the community, one should scrutinize characteristic attitudes of acting and being "jointly with others." *Primary emphasis should be placed on the attitudes of solidarity and opposition.*

Both of the labels *solidarity* and *opposition* get their meaning from their relationship to a commonality of action as well as the common good. Related to these labels is a certain qualifier, which, in the final analysis, is an ethical one. In our analysis, we will focus on the personalistic meaning of those two attitudes, and therefore their qualities will contain not so much their ethical meaning as a *pre-ethical* one. We are still primarily concerned with rendering a sketch of the very structure of human action and the values relevant to the accomplishment of an act. We are not primarily concerned with the value of the act stemming from a relationship to an ethical norm.

. . . *We desire to continue solely with the subjective accomplishment of acts and with their immanent value, which is a personalistic value.* In this context, we will find the key to the explanation for the proper dynamism of the self within the confines of a variety of communities of action and existence. For this reason, the categorization of attitudes that we intend to analyze will be primarily personalistic and, in that sense, *pre-ethical.* In this chapter (however) we are fully aware that we are proceeding on the border between ontology and ethics brought about by the axiological aspect—that means by the wealth of values that is difficult to exclude from an ontology of the self.

We will join the analysis of the attitudes of solidarity and opposition because each is needed to understand the other. The attitude of *solidarity* is a "natural" consequence of the fact that a human being exists and acts together with others. Solidarity is also the foundation of a community in which the common good conditions and liberates participation, and participation serves the common good, supports it, and implements it. Solidarity means the continuous readiness to accept and perform that part of a task which is imposed due to the participation as member of a specific community.

Because of solidarity, a person performs what is expected of him . . . "for the good of the whole"—thus, for the common good. . . . Solidarity, in a certain sense, prevents transgression into the field of someone else's obligation. . . . This attitude corresponds to the principle of participation because participation, *understood objectively and "materially," indicates certain common structures of human action and existence.* The attitude of solidarity respects the limits imposed by the structures and accepts the duties that are assigned to each member of the community. Assuming responsibility for a duty that has not been assigned to me is fundamentally contrary to the concepts of community and participation.

There are instances, however, when solidarity demands such a contrariness. In such instances, restricting oneself to the assigned duty only could be tantamount to a lack of solidarity. This is indirectly proven by the fact that in solidarity the attitude toward the common good has to be always present, active, and dominant to such an extent that a human being must know when he has to undertake the performance of a task that is beyond his usual action and responsibility. A specific sensitivity for the needs of the community . . . is expressed by the readiness to move beyond the partial and particularistic . . . , *the readiness to "complete" by my act that which others complete jointly.* This quality enters . . . into the very nature of participation—which we now understand subjectively as a quality of the self and not only objectively as a division of tasks that fall upon everyone in the cooperative structure of acting and existing. This is why it can be maintained that the basic expression of participation as a quality of the self is the attitude of solidarity. On the basis of this attitude, a human being finds the fulfillment of himself by adding to the fulfillment of others.

The attitude of solidarity, however, does not exclude the attitude of opposition. *Opposition is not a fundamental contradiction of solidarity.* One who expresses opposition does not remove himself from participation in the community, does not withdraw his readiness to act for the common good. Naturally, it is quite possible to have a different understanding of opposition. Here, however, we understand opposition basically as an attitude of solidarity. We understand it not as a negation of the common good or a denial of the need for participation, but as a confirmation of both. The content of opposition is primarily a method of understanding the common good and—most importantly—perceiving the way in which it is to be realized. Experience with diverse forms of opposition . . . teaches that people who oppose do not wish to leave the community because of their opposition. They are searching for their own place in the community—*they are searching for participation and such a definition of the common good that would permit them to participate more fully and effectively in the community.* There are countless examples of people quarreling—thus, assuming the attitude of opposition—precisely because they have in their hearts a concern for the common good, for example, parents who oppose their children because they want the best possible upbringing for them, or statesmen who oppose . . . because they are concerned with the good of a nation or a state, etc.

Perhaps these examples do not show the entire picture of opposition, but they point to it. The basis for opposition results from the personal view of the community and its common good. Opposition is also an expression of the vital need for participation in the community of existence, but especially in the community of action. Such an opposition has to be viewed as constructive. . . . We are concerned with such a structure of community that permits the emergence of opposition based on solidarity. Moreover, the structure must not only *allow the emergence of the opposition, give it the opportunity to express itself, but also must make it possible for the opposition to function for the good of the community.* . . . A human community only then has a correct structure when a rightful opposition not only possesses the right of citizenship but is also endowed with the potential for effectiveness needed by the common good and demanded by the right of participation.

It is evident . . . that the common good has to be perceived dynamically and not statically. The common good depends basically on solidarity, but it cannot close itself off or cut itself off from opposition. *It seems that the principle of dialogue is an effective countermeasure to a restrictive structure of a human community and participation.* The concept *dialogue* has many meanings. At this point, we emphasize only one—that which is applicable to the formation and deepening of human solidarity even through opposition. Opposition might make living and acting together more difficult but should neither ruin it nor render it impossible. A dialogue may lead to the comprehension of what is real in a given confrontational situation by eliminating the subjective attitudes and preferences of the participants in the dialogue. It is those elements that are the germs of infections, conflicts, and fights among people. Whatever is real and right always deepens the self and enriches the community. The principle of dialogue is so vital because it serves *to avoid tensions, conflicts, and fights,* which can be seen in so many communities. Moreover, dialogues *attempt to reveal what is real and right in those communities and could be a source of good for the people.* The principle of dialogue should be accepted regardless of the difficulties that emerge on the way to holding it.

Analysis of Attitudes: Inauthentic Attitudes

... In considering the possible loss of authenticity that threatens the attitudes of solidarity and opposition ..., *it is important to indicate here certain inauthentic attitudes.* We shall describe them through the use of labels that are rather more popular than scientific: These are *conformism* and *avoidance*.... Both of these attitudes are inauthentic for very basic reasons and not because they are simply deformations of solidarity and opposition.

... The label *conformism* denotes similarity and assimilation with others—a normal process and, under certain circumstances, even a positive one. Nonetheless, the concept *conformism,* despite its positive association, indicates something negative. *It indicates the absence of a basic solidarity and an avoidance of opposition.* When it indicates assimilation to others in the community, it does it only in external, superficial manifestations devoid of a personal reason, conviction, and election. Conformity primarily contains a certain surrender, a specific variety of apathy in which a human being is only the subject of a "happening" and not the instigator of his own attitude and his own engagement in the community. The human being does not create the community but somehow "allows himself" to be included in the collectivity. Hidden within conformity is a limitation—if not a denial—or at least a weakness of self-transcendence, self-determination, and selection.... We are not concerned here with a simple submission to others in a community. This could have, in many instances, a positive connotation. It is something else that concerns us here: It is a *basic resignation, a giving up of self-*

fulfillment in acting "jointly with others" and of acting itself. The human self agrees that the community takes the self away from him.

At the same time, the person takes himself away from the community. *Conformism is a denial of participation in the real meaning of that term.* Real participation is replaced by the illusion of participation. It is a superficial assimilation to others without conviction and without an authentic engagement. In that way the human capacity of creative structuring of a community is as if suspended or even counterfeited. This must have a negative consequence for the common good whose dynamism flows from real participation. Conformism means something opposite. It creates the condition of indifference for the common good. Conformism is a special variant of individualism. It is a flight from the community through the subterfuge of external posturing. Conformity is more like *uniformity* than unity. Under the surface of uniformity exist differentiations, and it befalls the community to create for it the conditions necessary for participation. Conformism is unacceptable. In a situation where people only externally assimilate or acquiesce to the demands of the community, and they do it only to avoid unpleasantnesses, the self and the community suffer irreplaceable losses.

The attitude we describe as avoidance *seems indifferent to illusions of being concerned with the common good, an attitude that was part of* conformism. In a certain sense, avoidance is more authentic, but basically it also suffers from inauthenticity. Conformism avoids opposition; avoidance avoids conformism. This, however, does not change avoidance into an authentic opposition to conformism. . . . Avoidance is only a retreat. Perhaps it is even a sign of protest but without an attempt at engagement. Avoidance is an absence of participation and therefore an absence from the community.

Avoidance can be expressed through absence. . . . In such instances, avoidance gives a human being a substitute method of not expressing solidarity or opposition. Since avoidance or absence can be consciously chosen, one cannot deny that it has a personalistic value. If, however, there are reasons that justify the attitude of avoidance, then the same reasons form an accusation of the community. The basic good of a community is the potential for participation. If participation is not possible—which explains the reason for avoidance—then the community does not properly function. It lacks a common good, thus avoidance or absence become venues of "exit" for the member of the community.

Despite all of these reasons that might rationalize avoidance as a *sui generis* substitute attitude, it still remains impossible to ascribe to it an authentic character in the area of acting and being "jointly with others."

. . . In conformism and avoidance, the human being is convinced *that the community is taking away his self, and that is why he attempts to take his self away from the community.* In the case of conformity, he does it by maintaining the appearances; in the attitude of avoidance, he seems not to care about appearances. In both instances, something very vital is taken out of the human being. It is that dynamic quality of the self that enables it to perform acts and authentically fulfills the self through these acts in the community of being and acting "jointly with others."

Membership and Closeness

. . . Membership in a community creates a system of behavior . . . which comes into very close contact with another system of great importance to [the understanding of participation]. This system is participation with someone who is very close. Membership in a community as a system and participation with someone very close are similar systems and interpenetrate each other, but are not identical. What we mean by the expression *someone very close* essentially differs from the concept *member of a community. Each of these terms indicates other possibilities as well as other directions for participation by the self.* In each, the social nature of man receives a different expression.

. . . The concepts *someone very close* and *member of a community or society* serve to classify behaviors that help us understand more clearly and all-inclusively the concept *participation. . . . The concept closeness indicates something deeper than proximity . . . between people.* And that is why it is more basic than the concept *member of a community,* even though the concept *membership* assumes closeness among people. Membership neither creates nor annihilates this fact. People become members of many communities . . . ; they become close to them or estranged from them, and that indicates a certain weakness of community, however they may remain very close or never cease being close.

. . . The concept *closeness* forces us to perceive and value in man something that is independent of membership in any community. It forces us to see and value something more unconditional. *The concept closeness is fused to a human being and, as such, to every value of the self regardless of any relationship to any kind of community or society.* The concept *closeness* takes under consideration—*or rather is solely concerned with—humanity,* whose owner is equally every other human being as "I" am. The concept *closeness* is the widest scope of community, reaching much further than any kind of *otherness,* and this includes membership in a variety of human communities. The concepts *membership, society,* and *community* assume the reality identified by closeness—but, at the same time, limit it and, in a way, push it into the background and veil it. Primary and at the forefront is the assimilation to a specific community; whereas, the notion *closeness* indicates the fundamental assimilation of people to themselves in humanity itself. Thus, the concept *closeness* indicates the most common reality and the most common general basis of community among people. *The community in humanity is the basis of all communities.* If any community is severed from this basic community, it must lose its humane and human character.

In this perspective we have to think through to the end the problem of participation. Until this point, we have been attempting to illuminate the meaning of participation based on every human being—every self—belonging to a variety of communities that reveal and confirm the social nature of the self. However, the capacity to participate reaches further: It reaches as far as is indicated by the concept *closeness.* The human self is capable not only of participating in existing and acting jointly with others but has the capacity of participating in the very humanity of others. Every participation in a community is simultaneously based and finds its personal meaning through the capability of participating in the humanity of every human being. This is what is indicated by the concept *closeness.*

. . . We are reaching the specific fullness of meaning of that reality which, from the beginning of this chapter, we described as *partici-*

pation. It is, however, necessary to warn at this time against the suggestion that the concept *closeness* and the concept *member of a community* mean something separate or contradictory.

We previously indicated their partial confluence, and now we intend to deepen this understanding. This basic confluence is confirmed by the *social nature of man,* although that also serves to explain and confirm the difference between closeness and membership. One should also guard against trying to understand the concept *closeness* as a system relevant to all inter-human relations. This same reservation holds true for membership in a community.

. . . *We are concerned here with the mutual interpenetration of subjects within the subjective dimension of participation. . . . The capacity of participation in humanity itself of every human being forms the core of all participation, and conditions the personalistic value of all acting and being "jointly with others."*

The Meaning of the Commandment to Love

For this reason, permit us to consecrate the final sentences of this book to the evangelical commandment to love. We have frequently emphasized that we do not intend to enter the field of ethics, and now we will stop on the threshhold of the strictly ethical commandment "you will love. . . ." We are not going to analyze the entire objective content of this commandment, and we especially refrain from analyzing the ethical meaning of love. We only wish to emphasize that this commandment, in a very clear, specific, and consequential manner, confirms that in any acting and being "jointly with others" the structure of the relationship *closeness* is of basic importance. The commandment reveals in a very specific and consequential way through a confrontation with the "I" the meaning "Love your neighbor as you love yourself." *The system of relationship to neighbor* (closeness) *gains its fundamental importance* among all the other systems ruling human communities *because it towers above them in the range of its simplicity and profundity.* It indicates a fullness in the concept *participation* that is absent from any membership in any kind of community. The system of relationships contained in the concept *closeness* finalizes all that is contained in any system that has the character of *membership in a community.* It is fundamentally higher. . . . The concept *closeness* indicates the assimilation of all people to the "I" on the basis of humanity itself, but the system of relationships indicated by membership in a community does not. One could even imply a certain transcendence in the concept *closeness* in relation to *member of a community.* All of this is implied in the evangelical commandment.

Of course, this should not be understood as posing some sort of limitation of communal values of human action and existence. Such an interpretation would be a deformation of the commandment. The commandment "you shall love" has a thoroughly communal character . . . and emphasizes what makes a community truly human. The commandment also explains why *the two concepts* closeness *and* membership in a community *should not be viewed as being either separate or opposite—but belong together.* This also is derived from the personalistic content of the evangelical commandment.

. . . From the point of view of participation, therefore, *one should eliminate the possibility of a mutual limitation by the two structures.* In acting and existing "jointly with others," both systems, *closeness* and *membership in a community,* should interpenetrate each other and complete each other. One cannot allow this separation because that would hide in itself the danger of basic alienation. The philosophies of the nineteenth and twentieth centuries understood by the term *alienation,* "an estrangement of a human being from his humanness," which is the same as the elimination of that very value that we described as *personalistic.* In the sphere of acting and being "jointly with others," the alienation can occur precisely when participation alone in a community hides and limits participation in the humanness of "others." Alienation occurs due to the weakening of the fundamental assimilation that gives a community of people its human dimension. Perhaps the view that the danger of dehumanization stems only from the structure of things was too one-sided: Nature, conditions of work, civilization are too narrow to account for it. Although, to a large extent, one cannot deny the accuracy of this thesis, it cannot be accepted as exclusive. Moreover, man is not the creator of nature but its master. He is, however, the creator of relations of production as well as of civilization. He can therefore prevent them from being dehumanizing and leading to alienation. Therefore, *at the root of all human alienation through structured relations transmitted by objects, we must posit alienation as stemming from man himself.* It seems that the commandment "you shall love" leads us to its essence. The root of alienation of human beings by human beings is contained in the neglect of the depth of participation contained in the subject, *closeness,* and the relevant assimilation of people in humanity as the basic community.

It is mandatory that in structuring human coexistence and cooperation on various levels and on the basis of a variety of ties that determine communities and societies the system of relationships identified as *closeness* be the final determinant. If any human community neglects this system of relations, then it condemns itself to a diminishing participation and to the creation of a precipice between the self and the community. This is not an indifferent kind of precipice but the precipice of destruction. . . . Here this truth shows its frightening face.

However, this is not the proper face. The commandment "you shall love" emphasizes the bright, shining side of reality of human action and existence. . . . The commandment to love defines the exact scope of duties and obligations that have to be assumed by all people—the self and the community—in order for all the good of acting and existing "jointly with others" to be truly realized.

3

Human Sexuality: The Theology of the Body

Nobody can be content with
moral perception in the abstract;
one must act in accordance with it.
FRANZ KAFKA

FOR nearly a year now John Paul II has been sharing with the throngs that come to hear him every Wednesday his thoughts about our human beginnings and our bodies. He views the body as composed not of separate attributes contained within one generalized structure, but as a unity with many ways of expressing itself.

The thoughts expressed by the Pope are a sophisticated summation of Love and Responsibility, *a work he began about twenty years ago and which will soon be available to the English-speaking world. The book reveals how deeply concerned Karol Wojtyla is with developing a fundamental understanding of human sexuality in all of its aspects and functions. The material we have gathered for this anthology however is the ripened fruit of those reflections. We have entitled this series of shared reflections published seriatim by* L'Osservatore Romano, *the official Vatican newspaper, "The Theology of the Body." Our justification is the frequent use of this phrase by John Paul II.*

In the context of a philosophy of praxis, a term used to describe man's interaction with his environment, the emphasis has always been placed on the nature or method of interaction and the impact on the "other"—the object of the "praxis." Karol Wojtyla places all of his emphasis on the "actor," the originator of the praxis—on man. The "theology of the body" is a personalistic approach to a philosophy which until now has suffered from an overly deterministic, materialistic, and objective-scientific approach.

But the first step to be taken, John Paul says, citing the opening chapters of Genesis is to understand our "beginnings." This understanding includes a deep comprehension of the very unique, very special meaning of our bodies in their relationship to God, loneliness, sex, shame, and knowledge.

I

From the point of view of biblical criticism, it is necessary to mention immediately that the *first account of man's creation is chronologically later than the second.* The origin of this latter is much more remote. This more ancient text is defined as "Yahwist" because the term "Yahweh" is used to denominate God. It is difficult not to be struck by the fact that the image of God presented there has quite considerable anthropomorphic traits (among others, we read in fact that ". . . the Lord God formed man of dust from the ground, and breathed into his nostrils the breath of life" (Gen.2:7).

In comparison with this description, the first account, that is, the one held to be chronologically later, is much more mature both as regards the image of God, and as regards the formulation of the essential truths about man. This account derives from the priestly and "Elohist" tradition, from "Elohim," the term used in that account for God.

Male and Female

Granted that in this narration man's creation as male and female—to which Jesus refers in his reply according to Matthew 19—is inserted into the seven-day cycle of the creation of the world, there could be attributed to it especially a cosmological character: man is created on earth together with the visible world. But at the same time the Creator orders him to subdue and have dominion over the earth (cf. Gen. 1:28): he is therefore placed over the world. Even though man is strictly bound to the visible world, nevertheless the biblical narrative does not speak of his likeness to the rest of creatures, but only to God ("God created man in his own image, in the image of God he created him . . ." Gen. 1:27). In the seven-day cycle of creation there is evident a precise graduated procedure.[1] Man, however, is not created according to a natural succession, but the Creator seems to halt before calling him into existence, as if he were pondering within himself to make a decision: "Let us make man in our image, after our likeness . . ." (Gen. 1:26).

Theological Character

The level of that first account of man's creation, even though chronologically later, is particularly of a theological character. An indication of that is especially the definition of man on the basis of his relationship with God ("in the image of God he created him"), which at the same time contains the affirmation of the absolute impossibility of reducing man to the "world." Already in the light of the first phrases of the Bible, man cannot be either understood or explained completely in terms of categories taken from the "world," that is, from the visible complex of bodies. Notwithstanding this, man also is corporeal. Genesis 1:27 observes that this essential truth about man refers both to the male and the female: "God created man in his image . . . male and female he created them."[2]

It must be recognized that the first account is concise, and free from any trace whatsoever of subjectivism. It contains only the objective facts and defines the objective reality, both when it speaks of man's creation, male and female, in the image of God, and when it adds a little later the words of the first blessing: "Be fruitful and multiply, and fill the earth; subdue it and have dominion over it" (Gen.1:28).

Inspiration for Thinkers

The first account of man's creation, which, as we observed, is of a theological nature, conceals within itself a powerful metaphysical content. Let it not be forgotten that this very text of the Book of Genesis has become the source of the most profound inspiration for thinkers who have sought to understand "being" and "existence" (perhaps only the third chapter of Exodus can bear comparison with this text).[3] Notwithstanding certain detailed and plastic expressions of the passage, man is defined there, first of all, in the dimensions of being and of existence (*esse*). He is defined in a way that is more metaphysical than physical.

To this mystery of creation ("in the image of God he created him") there corresponds the perspective of procreation ("Be fruitful and multiply, fill the earth"), of that becoming in the world and in time, of that *fieri* which is necessarily bound up with the metaphysical situation of creation: of contingent being (*contingens*). Precisely in this metaphysical context of the description of Genesis 1, it is necessary to understand the entity of the good, namely, the aspect of value. Indeed, this aspect appears in the cycle of nearly all of the days of creation and reaches its culmination after the creation of man: "God saw everything that he had made, and behold, it was very good" (Gen.1:31). For this reason it can be said with certainty that the first chapter of Genesis has established an unassailable point of reference and a solid basis for a metaphysic and also for an anthropology and an ethic, according to which "*ens et bonum convertuntur*" (being and the good are convertible). Undoubtedly, all this has a significance also for theology and especially for the theology of the body.

II

The second chapter of Genesis constitutes, in a certain manner, the most ancient description and record of man's self-knowledge, and together with the third chapter it is the first testimony of human conscience. A reflection in depth on this text—through the whole archaic form of the narrative, which manifests its primitive mythical character[4]—provides us *in nucleo* with nearly all the elements of the analysis of man, to which modern, and especially contemporary, philosophical anthropology is sensitive. It could be said that Genesis 2 presents the creation of man especially in its subjective aspect. Comparing both accounts, we arrive at the conclusion that this subjectivity corresponds to the objective reality of man created "in the image of God." This fact, also, is—in another way—important for the theology of the body, as we shall see in subsequent analyses.

First Human Being

It is significant that Christ, in his reply to the Pharisees, in which he appealed to the "beginning," indicates first of all the creation of man by referring to Genesis 1:27: "The Creator from the beginning created them male and female"; only afterwards does he quote the text of Genesis 2:24. The words which directly describe the unity and indissolubility of marriage are found *in the immediate context of the second account of creation*, whose characteristic feature is the separate creation of woman (cf. Gen.2:18–23), while the account of the creation of the first man is found in Genesis 2:5–7.

The first human being the Bible calls "Man" (*'adam*), but from the moment of the creation of the first woman, it begins to call him "man" (*'ish*), in relation to *'ishshah* ("woman," because she was taken from the man = *'ish*).[5]

It is also significant that Christ, in referring to Genesis 2:24, *not only links the "beginning" with the mystery of creation, but also leads us, one might say, to the limit of man's primitive innocence and of original sin.* The second description of man's creation is placed by the Book of Genesis precisely in this context. There we read first of all: "And the rib which the Lord God had taken from the man he made into a woman and brought her to the man; then the man said: 'this at last is bone of my bones and flesh of my flesh; she shall be called Woman, because she was taken out of Man' " (Gen. 2:22–23). "Therefore a man leaves his father and his mother and cleaves to his wife, and they become one flesh" (Gen. 2:24). "And the man and his wife were both naked, and they were not ashamed" (Gen. 2:25).

Tree of Knowledge

Immediately after these verses, Chapter 3 begins with its account of the first fall of the man and the woman, linked with the mysterious tree already called the "tree of the knowledge of good and evil" (Gen. 2:17). Thus there emerges an entirely new situation, essentially different from the preceding. The tree of the knowledge of good and evil is the line of demarcation between the two original situations of which the Book of Genesis speaks.

The first situation was that of original innocence, in which man (male and female) is, as it were, outside the sphere of the knowledge of good and evil, until the moment when he transgresses the Creator's prohibition and eats the fruit of the tree of knowledge. The second situation, however, is that in which man, after having disobeyed the Creator's command at the prompting of the evil spirit, symbolized by the serpent, finds himself, in a certain way, within the sphere of the knowledge of good and evil. This second situation determines the state of human sinfulness, in contrast to the state of primitive innocence.

Even though the "Yahwist" text is, all in all, very concise, nevertheless it suffices to differentiate *and to set against each other with clarity those two original situations.* We speak here of situations, having before our eyes the account which is a description of events. Nonetheless, by means of this description and all its particulars, there emerges the essential difference between the state of man's sinfulness and that of his original innocence.[6]

Systematic theology will discern in these two antithetical situations two different states of human nature: *the state of integral nature* and *the state of fallen nature.* All this emerges from that "Yahwist" text of Genesis 2 and 3, which contains in itself the most ancient word of revelation, and evidently has a fundamental significance for the theology of man and for the theology of the body.

The "Yahwist" Text

When Christ, referring to the "beginning," directs his questioners to the words written in Genesis 2:24, he orders them, in a certain sense, to go beyond the boundary which, in the "Yahwist" text of Genesis, runs between the first and second situation of man. He does not approve what Moses had permitted "for their hardness of heart," and he appeals to the words of the first divine regulation, which in this text is expressly linked to man's state of original innocence. This means that this regulation has not lost its force, even though man has lost his primitive innocence.

Christ's reply is decisive and unequivocal. Therefore we must draw from it the normative conclusions which have an essential significance not only for ethics, but especially for the theology of man and for the theology of the body, which as a particular element of theological anthropology is constituted on the basis of the word of God which is revealed.

III

The analysis of the relative passages in the Book of Genesis (chap. 2) has already brought us to surprising conclusions which concern the anthropology, that is, the fundamental science about man, contained in this Book. In fact, in relatively few sentences, the ancient text portrays man as *a person with the subjectivity that characterizes him.*

When God-Yahweh gives this first man, so formed, the order that concerns all the trees that grow in the "garden in Eden," particularly the tree of the knowledge of good and evil, there is added to the features of the man, described above, the moment of choice and self-determination, that is, of free will. In this way, the image of man, as a person endowed with a subjectivity of his own, appears before us, as it were, completed in his first outline.

In the concept of original solitude are included both self-consciousness and self-determination. The fact that man is "alone" conceals within it this ontological structure and is at the same time an indication of true comprehension. Without that, we cannot understand correctly the subsequent words, which constitute the prelude to the creation of the first woman: "I will make a helper." But above all, without that deep significance of man's original solitude, it is not possible to understand and interpret correctly the whole situation of man, created "in the image of God," which is the situation of the first, or rather original, Covenant with God.

Partner of the Absolute

This man, about whom the narrative in the first chapter says that he was created "in the image of God," is manifested in the second narrative *as subject of the Covenant,* that is, a subject constituted as a person, constituted in the dimension of "*partner of the Absolute*" since he must consciously discern and choose between good and evil, between life and death. The words of the first order of God-

Yahweh (Gen. 2:16–17), which speak directly of the submission and dependence of man-the-creature on his Creator, indirectly reveal precisely this level of humanity, as subject of the Covenant and "partner of the Absolute." *Man is "alone": that means that he, through his own humanity,* through what he is, is constituted at the same time in a *unique, exclusive and unrepeatable relationship with God himself.* The anthropological definition contained in the Yahwist text approaches, on its part, what is expressed in the theological definition of man, which we find in the first narrative of creation ("Let us make man in our image, after our likeness": Gen. 1:26).

Conscious of Being "Alone"

Man, thus formed, belongs to the visible world, he is a body among bodies. Taking up again and, in a way, reconstructing, the meaning of original solitude, we apply it to man in his totality. His body, through which man participates in the visible created world, makes him at the same time conscious of being "alone." Otherwise he would not have been able to arrive at that conviction, which, in fact, as we read, he reached (cf. Gen. 2:20), if his body had not helped him to understand it, making the matter evident. Consciousness of solitude might have been shattered precisely because of his body itself. The man, *'adam,* might have reached the conclusion, on the basis of the experience of his own body, that he was substantially similar to other living beings (*animalia*). But, on the contrary, as we read, he did not arrive at this conclusion, in fact he reached the conviction that he was "alone." The Yahwist text never speaks directly of the body; even when it says that "the Lord God formed man of dust from the ground," it speaks of man and not of his body. Nevertheless the narrative taken as a whole offers us a sufficient basis to perceive this man, created in the visible world, precisely as a body among bodies.

The analysis of the Yahwist text also enables us to *link man's original solitude with consciousness of the body* through which man is distinguished from all the *animalia* and "is separated" from them, and also *through which* he is a *person.* It can be affirmed with certainty that that man, thus formed, has at the same time consciousness and awareness of the meaning of his own body. And that on the basis of the experience of original solitude.

Meaning of his Corporality

All that can be considered as an implication of the second narrative of the creation of man, and the analysis of the text enables us to develop it amply.

When at the beginning of the Yahwist text, even before it speaks of the creation of man from "dust of the ground," we read that "there was no one to till the land or to make channels of water spring out of the earth to irrigate the whole land" (Gen. 2:5–6), we rightly associate this passage with the one in the first narrative, in which God's command is expressed: "Fill the earth and subdue it: and have dominion . . ." (Gen. 1:28). The second narrative alludes specifically *to the work that man carries out* to till the earth. The first fundamental means to dominate the earth lies in man himself. Man can dominate the earth because he alone—and no other of the living beings—is capable of "tilling it" and transforming it according to his own needs ("he made channels of water spring out of the earth to irrigate the whole land"). And lo, this first outline of a specifically human activity seems to belong to the definition of man, as it emerges from the analysis of the Yahwist text. Consequently, it can be affirmed that this outline is intrinsic to the meaning of the original solitude and belongs *to that dimension of solitude, through which man, from the beginning, is in the visible world as a body among bodies and discovers the meaning of his own corporality.*

The words of the book of Genesis, "It is not good that the man should be alone" (2:18), are, as it were, a prelude to the narrative of the creation of woman. Together with this narrative, the sense of original solitude becomes part of the meaning of original unity, the key point of which seems to be precisely the words of Genesis 2:24, to which Christ refers in his talk with the Pharisees: "A man shall leave his father and mother and be joined to his wife, and the two shall become one flesh" (Mt. 19:5). If Christ, referring to the "beginning," quotes these words, it is opportune for us to clarify the meaning of that original unity, which has its roots in the fact of the creation of man as male and female.

The narrative of the first chapter of Genesis does not know the problem of man's original solitude: Man, in fact, is "male and female" right from the beginning. The Yahwist text of the second chapter, on the contrary, authorizes us, in a way, to think first only of the man since, by means of the body, he belongs to the visible world, but goes beyond it; then, it makes us think of the same man, but through the dualism of sex.

Corporality and sexuality are not completely identified. Although the human body, in its normal constitution, bears within it the signs of sex and is, by its nature, male or female, *the fact, however, that man is a "body" belongs to the structure of the personal subject more deeply than the fact that he is in his somatic constitution also male or female.* Therefore the meaning of original solitude, which can be referred simply to "man," is substantially prior to the meaning of original unity. The latter, in fact, is based on masculinity and femininity, as if on two different "incarnations," that is, on two ways of "being a body" of the same human being, created "in the image of God" (Gen. 1:27).

Dialogue between Man and God-Creator

Following the Yahwist text, in which the creation of woman was described separately (Gen. 2:21–22), we must have before our eyes, at the same time, that "image of God" of the first narrative of creation. The second narrative keeps, in language and in style, all the characteristics of the Yahwist text. The way of narrating agrees with the way of thinking and expressing oneself of the period to which the text belongs.

It can be said, following the contemporary philosophy of religion and that of language, that the language in question is a mythical one. In this case, in fact, the term "myth" does not designate a fabulous content, but merely an archaic way of expressing a deeper content. Without any difficulty, we discover, under the layer of the ancient narrative, that content, which is really marvellous as regards the qualities and the condensation of the truths contained in it.

Let us add that the second narrative of the creation of man keeps, up to a certain point, the form of a dialogue between man and God-Creator, and that is manifested above all *in that stage in which man* ('adam) *is definitively created as male and female* ('ish-'ishshah).[7] The creation takes place almost simultaneously in two dimensions; the action of God-Yahweh who creates occurs in correlation with the process of human consciousness.

So, therefore, God-Yahweh says: "It is not good that the man should be alone; I will make him a helper fit for him" (Gen. 2:18). At the same time the man confirms his own solitude (Gen. 2:20). Next we read: "So the Lord God caused a deep sleep to fall upon the man, and while he slept took one of his ribs and closed up its place with flesh; and the rib which the Lord God had taken from the man he made into a woman" (Gen. 2:21–22). Taking into consideration the specificity of the language, it must be recognized in the first place that that sleep in the Genesis account in which the man is immersed, thanks to God-Yahweh, in preparation for the new creative act, gives us food for thought.

Against the background of contemporary mentality, accustomed—through analysis of the subconscious—to connecting sexual contents with the world of dreams, that sleep may bring forth a particular association.[8] However, the Bible narrative seems to go beyond the dimension of man's subconscious. If we admit, moreover, a significant difference of vocabulary, we can conclude that the man (*'adam*) falls into that "sleep" in order to wake up "male" and "female." In fact, for the first time in Genesis 2:23 we come across the distinction *'ish-'ishshah*. Perhaps, therefore, the *analogy of sleep* indicates here not so much a passing from consciousness to subconsciousness, as a specific return to non-being (sleep contains an element of annihilation of man's conscious existence), that is, to the moment preceding the creation, *in order that, through God's creative initiative, solitary "man" may emerge from it again* in his double unit as male and female.[9]

In any case, in the light of the context of Genesis 2:18-20, there is no doubt that man falls into that "sleep" with the desire of finding a being like himself. If, by analogy with sleep, we can speak here also of a dream, we must say that that biblical archetype allows us to admit as the content of that dream a "second self," which is also personal and equally referred to the situation of original solitude, that is, to the whole of that process of the stabilization of human identity in relation to living beings (*animalia*) as a whole, since it is the process of man's "differentiation" from this environment. In this way, the circle of the solitude of the man-person is broken, because the first "man" awakens from his sleep as "male and female."

The Same Humanity

The woman is made "with the rib" that God-Yahweh had taken from the man. Considering the archaic, metaphorical and figurative way of expressing the thought, we can establish that it is a question here of homogeneity of the whole being of both. This homogeneity concerns above all the body, the somatic structure, and is confirmed also by the man's first words to the woman who has been created: "This at last is bone of my bones and flesh of my flesh" (Gen. 2:23). And yet the words quoted refer also to the humanity of the male-man. They must be read in the context of the affirmations made before the creation of the woman, in which, although the "incarnation" of the man does not yet exist, she is defined as "a helper fit for him" (cf. Gen. 2:18 and 2:20). In this way, therefore, the *woman is created, in a sense, on the basis of the same humanity.*

Somatic homogeneity, in spite of the difference in constitution bound up with the sexual difference, is so evident that the man (male), on waking up from the genetic sleep, expresses it at once, when he says: "This at last is bone of my bones and flesh of my flesh; she shall be called Woman, because she was taken out of Man" (Gen. 2:23). In this way the man (male) manifests for the first time joy and even exaltation, for which he had no reason before, owing to the lack of a being like himself. Joy in the other human being, in the second "self," dominates in the words spoken by the man (male) on seeing the woman (female). All that helps to establish the full meaning of original unity. The words here are few, but each one is of great weight. We must therefore take into account—and we will do so also later—the fact that that first woman, "made with the rib . . . taken from the man (male)," is at once accepted as a fit helper for him.

IV

On the basis of the analyses carried out up to now, we have already been able to realize that what we called at the beginning "revelation of the body," helps us somehow to discover the extraordinary side of what is ordinary. That is possible because the revelation (the original one, which found expression first in the Yahwist account of

Gen. 2–3, then in the text of Gen. 1) takes into consideration precisely these primordial experiences in which appears almost completely the absolute originality of what the male-female human being is: as a man, that is, also through his body. Man's experience of his body, as we discover it in the biblical text quoted, is certainly on the threshold of the whole subsequent "historical" experience. It also seems to rest, however, at such an ontological depth that man does not perceive it in his own everyday life, even if at the same time, and in a certain way, he presupposes it and postulates it as part of the process of formation of his own image.

Without this introductory reflection, it would be impossible to define the meaning of original nakedness and tackle the analysis of Genesis 2:25, which runs as follows: "And the man and his wife were both naked, and were not ashamed." At first sight, this detail, apparently a secondary one, in the Yahwist account of man's creation, may seem something inadequate or misplaced. One would think that the passage quoted cannot bear comparison with what has been dealt with in the preceding verses and that, in a way, it goes beyond the context. However, this judgment does not stand up to a deeper analysis. In fact, Genesis 2:25 presents one of the key-elements of the original revelation, as decisive as the other texts of Genesis (2:20 and 2:23), which have already enabled us to define the meaning of man's original solitude and original unity. To these is added, as the third element, the meaning of original nakedness, clearly stressed in the context; and, in the first biblical draft of anthropology, it is not something accidental. On the contrary, it is precisely the key for its full and complete understanding.

It is evident that precisely this element of the ancient biblical text makes a specific contribution to the theology of the body, a contribution that absolutely cannot be ignored. Further analyses will confirm this. But, before undertaking them, I take the liberty of pointing out that the very text of Genesis 2:25 expressly requires that the reflections on the theology of the body should be connected with the dimension of man's personal subjectivity; it is within the latter, in fact, that consciousness of the meaning of the body develops. Genesis 2:25 speaks about it far more directly than other parts of that Yahwist text, which we have already defined as the first recording of human consciousness.

The sentence, according to which the first human beings, man and woman, "were naked" and yet "were not ashamed," unquestionably describes their state of consciousness, in fact, their mutual experience of the body, that is, the experience on the part of the man of the femininity that is revealed in the nakedness of the body and, reciprocally, the similar experience of masculinity on the part of the woman. By saying that "they were not ashamed," the author tries to describe this mutual experience of the body with the greatest precision possible for him. It can be said that this type of precision reflects a basic experience of man in the "common" and pre-scientific sense, but it also corresponds to the requirements of anthropology and in particular of contemporary anthropology, which likes to refer to so-called fundamental experiences such as the experience of shame.[10]

Referring here to the precision of the account, such as was possible for the author of the Yahwist text, we are led to consider the degrees of experience of "historical" man, laden with the inheritance of sin, degrees, however, which methodically start precisely from the state of original innocence. Previously we have already seen that, referring to "the beginning" (which we have subjected here to successive contextual analyses) Christ indirectly establishes the idea of continuity and connection between those two states, as if allowing us to move back from the threshold of man's "historical" sinfulness to his original innocence. Precisely Genesis 2:25 makes it particularly necessary to cross that threshold.

It is easy to point out how this passage, together with the meaning of original nakedness inherent in it, takes its place in the contextual setting of the Yahwist narrative. After some verses, in fact, the same author writes: "Then the eyes of both were opened, and they knew that they were naked; and they sewed fig leaves together and made themselves aprons" (Gen. 3:7). This new moment or new situation also implies a new content and a new quality of experience of the body, so that it can no longer be said: "they were naked, but were not ashamed." *Here, therefore, shame is an experience that is not only original, but a "boundary" one.*

The difference of formulations, that divides Genesis 2:25 from Genesis 3:7, is, therefore, a significant one. In the first case, "they were naked, but they were not ashamed"; in the second case, "they knew that they were naked." Does that mean that, to begin with, "they did not know that they were naked"? That they did not see the nakedness of each other's body? The significant change testified by the biblical text about the experience of shame (of which Genesis speaks again, particularly in 3:10–12), takes place at a deeper level than the pure and simple use of the sense of sight.

A comparative analysis between Genesis 2:25 and Genesis 3 leads necessarily to the conclusion that it is not a question here of passing from "not knowing" to "knowing," but of a radical change of the meaning of the original nakedness of the woman before the man and of the man before the woman. It emerges from their conscience, as a fruit of the tree of the knowledge of good and evil: "Who told you that you were naked? Have you eaten of the tree of which I commanded you not to eat?" (Gen. 3:11).

This change directly concerns the experience of the meaning of one's body before the Creator and creatures. That this confirmed subsequently by the man's words: "I heard the sound of thee in the garden, and I was afraid, because I was naked; and I hid myself" (Gen. 3:10). But in particular that change, which the Yahwist text portrays so concisely and dramatically, concerns directly, perhaps in the most direct way possible, the man-woman, femininity-masculinity relationship.

V

What is shame and how can we explain its absence in the state of original innocence, in the very depth of the mystery of the creation of man as male and female? From contemporary analyses of shame—and in particular sexual modesty—we can deduce the complexity of this fundamental experience, in which man expresses himself as a person according to his own specific structure. In the experience of shame, the human being experiences fear with regard to his "second self" (as, for example, woman before man), and this is substantially fear for his own "self." With shame, the human being manifests almost "instinctively" the need of affirmation and acceptance of this "self," according to its rightful value. He experiences it at the same time both within himself, and externally, before the "other." It can therefore be said that shame is a complex experience also in the sense that, almost keeping one human being away from the other (woman from man), it seeks at the same time to draw them closer personally, creating a suitable basis and level in order to do so.

For the same reason, it has a fundamental significance as regards the formation of *ethos* in human society, and in particular in the man-woman relationship. The analysis of shame clearly indicates how deeply it is rooted precisely in mutual relations, how exactly it expresses the essential rules for the "communion of persons," and likewise how deeply it touches the dimension of man's original "solitude." The appearance of "shame" in the subsequent biblical narration of Chapter 3 of Genesis has a pluridimensional significance, and it will be opportune to resume the analysis of it in due time.

What does its original absence mean, on the other hand, in Genesis 2:25: "They were both naked and were not ashamed"?

Misleading Analogies

It is necessary to establish, in the first place, that it is a question of a real non-presence of shame, and not a lack of underdevelopment of it. We cannot in any way sustain here a "primitivization" of its meaning. Therefore the text of Genesis 2:25 does not exclude decisively the possibility of thinking of a "lack of shame" or immodesty, but even more excludes the possibility of explaining it by means of analogy with some positive human experiences, such as for example those of childhood or of the life of so-called primitive peoples. These analogies are not only insufficient, but they can even be misleading. The words of Genesis 2:25, "they were not ashamed," do not express a lack, but, on the contrary, serve to indicate a particular fullness of consciousness and experience, above all fullness of understanding of the meaning of the body, bound up with the fact that "they were naked."

That this is how the text quoted is to be understood and interpreted, is testified by the continuation of the Yahwist narrative, in which the appearance of shame, and in particular of sexual modesty, is connected with the loss of that original fullness. Taking, therefore, the experience of shame as a "borderline" experience, and in particular to what fullness of understanding of the meaning of the body, the meaning of original nakedness, of which Genesis 2:25 speaks, corresponds.

Fullness of Consciousness

To answer this question, it is necessary to keep in mind the analytical process carried out so far, which has its basis in the Yahwist passage as a whole. In this context, man's original solitude is manifested as "non-identification" of his own humanity with the world of living beings (*animalia*) that surround him.

This "non-identification," following upon the creation of man as male and female, makes way for the happy discovery of one's own humanity "with the help" of the other human being; thus the man recognizes and finds again his own humanity "with the help" of the woman (Gen. 2:25). At the same time, this act of theirs realizes a perception of the world, which is carried out directly through the body ("flesh of my flesh"). It is the direct and visible source of the experience that arrives at establishing their unity in humanity. It is not difficult to understand, therefore, that nakedness corresponds to that fullness of consciousness of the meaning of the body, deriving from the typical perception of the senses.

One can think of this fullness in categories of truth of being or of reality, and it can be said that man and woman were originally given to each other precisely according to this truth since "they were naked." In the analysis of the meaning of original nakedness, this dimension absolutely cannot be disregarded. This participating in perception of the world—in its "exterior" aspect—is a direct and almost spontaneous fact, prior to any "critical" complication of knowledge and of human experience and is seen as closely connected with the experience of the meaning of the human body. The original innocence of "knowledge" could already be perceived in this way.

Meaning of Communication

However, it is not possible to determine the meaning of original nakedness considering only man's participation in exterior perception of the world; it is not possible to establish it without going down into the depths of man. Genesis 2:25 introduces us specifically to this level and wants us to seek there the original innocence of knowing. In fact, it is with the dimension of human inferiority that it is necessary to explain and measure that particular fullness of interpersonal communication, thanks to which man and woman "were naked and were not ashamed."

The concept of "communication," in our conventional language, has been practically alienated from its deepest, original semantic matrix. It is connected mainly with the sphere of the media, that is, for the most part, products that serve for understanding, exchange, and bringing closer together. It can be supposed, on the other hand, that, in its original and deeper meaning, "communication" was and is directly connected with subjects, who "communicate" precisely on the basis of the "common union" that exists between them, both to reach and to express a reality that is peculiar and pertinent only to the sphere of person-subjects.

In this way, the human body acquires a completely new meaning, which cannot be placed on the plane of the remaining "external" perception of the world. It expresses, in fact, the person in his ontological and existential concreteness, which is something more than the "individual," and therefore expresses the personal human "self," which derives its "exterior" perception from within.

Seeing Each Other

"Nakedness" signifies the original good of God's vision. It signifies all the simplicity and fullness of the vision through which the "pure" value of humanity as male and female, the "pure" value of the body and of sex, is manifested. The situation that is indicated, in such a concise and at the same time inspiring way, by the original revelation of the body as seen in particular by Genesis 2:25, does not know an interior rupture and opposition between what is spiritual and what is sensible, just as it does not know a rupture and opposition between what constitutes the person humanly and what in man is determined by sex: what is male and female.

Seeing each other, as if through the very mystery of creation, man and woman see each other even more fully and distinctly than through the sense of sight itself, that is, through the eyes of the body. They see and know each other, in fact, with all the peace of the interior gaze, which creates precisely the fullness of the intimacy of persons.

Gift for Each Other

If "shame" brings with it a specific limitation in seeing by means of the eyes of the body, this takes place above all because personal intimacy is, as it were, disturbed and almost "threatened" by this sight. According to Genesis 2:25, the man and the woman "were not ashamed": seeing and knowing each other in all the peace and tranquillity of the interior gaze, they "communicate" in the fullness of humanity, which is manifested in them as reciprocal complementariness precisely because they are "male" and "female." At the same time, they "communicate" on the basis of that communion of persons in which, through femininity and masculinity, they become a gift for each other. In this way they reach in reciprocity a special understanding of the meaning of their own body.

The original meaning of nakedness corresponds to that simplicity and fullness of vision, in which understanding of the meaning of the body comes about, as it were, at the very heart of their community-communion. We will call it "nuptial." The man and the woman in Genesis 2:23–25 emerge, precisely at the "beginning," with this consciousness of the meaning of their body. That deserves a careful analysis.

Bearing a Divine Image

If the narrative of the creation of man in the two versions, the Elohist and the Yahwist, enables us to establish the original meaning of solitude, unity and nakedness, it thereby enables us also to find ourselves on the ground of an adequate anthropology, which tries to understand and interpret man in what is essentially human.[11]

The Bible texts contain the essential elements of this anthropology, which are manifested in the theological context of the "image of God." This concept conceals within it the very root of the truth about man, revealed through that "beginning," to which Christ refers in the talk with the Pharisees (cf. Mt. 19:3–9), when he treats of the creation of human male and female. It must be recalled that all the analyses we make here are connected, at least indirectly, precisely with these words of his. Man, whom God created "male and female," bears the divine image imprinted on his body "from the beginning"; man and woman constitute, as it were, two different ways of the human "being of body" in the unity of that image.

Now, it is opportune to turn again to those fundamental words which Christ used, that is, the word "created" and the subject "Creator," introducing in the considerations made so far a new dimension, a new criterion of understanding and interpretation, which we will call "hermeneutics of the gift." The dimension of the gift decides the essential truth and depth of meaning of the original solitude-unity-nakedness. It is also at the very heart of the mystery of creation, which enables us to construct the theology of the body "from the beginning," but demands, at the same time, that we should construct it just in this way.

Relationship Emerges

The reading of the first chapter of the Book of Genesis introduces us to the mystery of creation, that is, the beginning of the world by the will of God, who is omnipotence and love. Consequently, every creature bears within him the sign of the original and fundamental gift.

At the same time, however, the concept of "giving" cannot refer to a nothingness. It indicates the one who gives and the one who receives the gift, and also the relationship that is established between them. Now, this relationship emerges in the account of creation at the very moment of the creation of man. This relationship is manifested above all by the expression: "God created man in his own image, in the image of God he created him" (Gen. 1:27).

In the narrative of the creation of the visible world, the giving has a meaning only with regard to man. In the whole work of creation, it can be said only of him that a gift was conferred on him: the visible world was created "for him." The biblical account of creation offers us sufficient reasons to understand and interpret in this way: creation is a gift, because there appears in it man who, as the "image of God," is capable of understanding the very meaning of gift in the call from nothingness to existence. And he is capable of answering the Creator with the language of this understanding. Interpreting the narrative of creation with this language, it can thus be deduced that creation constitutes the fundamental and original gift: man appears in creation as the one who received the world as a gift, and *vice versa* it can also be said the world received man as a gift.

VI

Rereading and analyzing the second narrative of creation, that is, the Yahwist text, we must ask ourselves if the first "man" (*'adam*), in his original solitude, really "lived" the world as a gift, with an attitude in conformity with the actual condition of one who has received a gift as is seen from the narrative in the first chapter. The second narrative shows us man, in fact, in the garden of Eden (cf. Gen. 2:8) but we must observe that, though in this situation of original happiness, the Creator himself (God Yahweh) and then also "man," instead of stressing the aspect of the world as a subjectively beautifying gift created for man (cf. the first narrative and in particular Gen. 26:29), point out that man is "alone."

We have already analysed the meaning of original solitude. Now, however, it is necessary to note that there clearly appears for the first time a certain lack of good: "It is not good that man (male) should be alone"—God-Yahweh says—"I will make him a helper . . ." (Gen. 2:18). The first "man" says the same thing. He, too, after having become thoroughly aware of his own solitude among all living beings on earth, waits for "a helper fit for him" (cf. Gen. 2:20). In fact, none of these beings (*animalia*) offers man the basic conditions which make it possible to exist in a relationship of mutual giving.

With and for Some One

In this way, therefore, these two expressions, namely, the adjective "alone" and the noun "helper," seem to be really the key to understand the very essence of the gift at the level of man, as existential content contained in the truth of the "image of God." In fact the gift reveals, so to speak, a particular characteristic of personal existence, or rather, of the very essence of the person. When God Yahweh says that "it is not good that man should be alone" (Gen. 2:18), he affirms that "alone," man does not completely realize this essence. He realizes it only by existing "*with some one*"—and even more deeply and completely: by existing "*for some one.*"

This norm of existence as a person is shown in the Book of Genesis as characteristic of creation, precisely by means of the meaning of these two words: "alone" and "helper." It is precisely these words which indicate as fundamental and constitutive for man both the relationship and the communion of persons. The communion of persons means existing in a mutual "for," in a relationship of mutual gift. And this relationship is precisely the fulfilment of "man's" original solitude.

Effected by Love

This fulfilment is, in its origin, beautifying. It is certainly implicit in man's original happiness, and constitutes precisely that happiness which belongs to the mystery of creation effected by love, which belongs to the very essence of creative giving. When man "the male," awakening from the sleep of Genesis, sees man, "the female," drawn from him he says: "This at last is bone of my bones and flesh of my flesh" (Gen. 2:23). These words express, in a way, the subjectively beautifying beginning of man's existence in the world. Since it took place at the "beginning," this confirms the process of individuation of man in the world, and springs, so to speak, from the very depths of his human solitude, which he lives as a person in presence of all other creatures and all living beings (*animalia*).

This "beginning" belongs, therefore, to an adequate anthropology and can always be verified on the basis of the latter. This purely anthropological verification brings us, at the same time, to the subject of the "person" and to the subject of the "body-sex." This simultaneousness is essential. If, in fact, we deal with sex without the person, the whole adequacy of the anthropology, which we find in the Book of Genesis, would be destroyed. And for our theological study the essential light of the revelation of the body, which appears so fully in these first affirmations, would then be veiled.

Body Expresses Person

There is a deep connection between the mystery of creation, as a gift springing from love, and that beautifying "beginning" of the existence of man as male and female, in the whole truth of their body and their sex, which is the pure and simple truth of communion between persons. When the first man exclaims, at the sight of the woman: "This is bone of my bones, and flesh of my flesh" (Gen. 2:23), he merely affirms the human identity of both. Exclaiming in this way, he seems to say: here is a body *that expresses the "person"*!

Following a preceding passage of the Yahwist text, it can also be said that this "body" reveals the "living soul," such as man became when God Yahweh breathed life into him (cf. Gen. 2:7), as a result of which there began his solitude before all other living beings. Precisely by traversing the depth of that original solitude, man now emerges in the dimension of the mutual gift, the expression of which—and for that very reason the expression of his existence as a person—is the human body in all the original truth of its masculinity and femininity.

The body, which expresses femininity, manifests the reciprocity and communion of persons. It expresses it by means of the gift as the fundamental characteristic of personal existence. This is the body: a witness to creation as a fundamental gift, and so a witness to Love as the source from which this same giving springs. Masculinity-femininity—namely, sex—is the original sign of a creative donation and of an awareness on the part of man, male-female, of a gift lived, so to speak, in an original way. Such is the meaning with which sex enters the theology of the body.

Genesis 2:24 speaks of the finality of man's masculinity and femininity, in the life of the spouses-parents. Uniting with each other so closely as to become "one flesh," they will subject, in a way, their humanity to the blessing of fertility, namely, "procreation," of which the first narrative speaks (Gen. 1:28). Man comes "into being" with consciousness of this finality of his own masculinity-femininity, that is, of his own sexuality. At the same time, the words of Genesis 2:25: "they were both naked, and were not ashamed," seem to add to this fundamental truth of the meaning of the human body, of its masculinity and femininity, another no less essential and fundamental truth. Man, aware of the procreative capacity of his body and of his sexuality, is at the same time free from the "constraint" of his own body and sex.

That original nakedness, mutual, and at the same time not weighed down by shame, expresses this interior freedom of man. Is this what freedom from the "sexual instinct" is? The concept of "instinct" already implies an interior constraint, similar to the instinct that stimulates fertility and procreation in the whole world of living beings (*animalia*). It seems, however, that both texts of the Book of Genesis, the first and the second narrative of the creation of man, connected sufficiently the perspective of procreation with the fundamental characteristic of human existence in the personal sense. Consequently the analogy of the human body and of sex in relation to the world of animals—which we can call analogy "of nature"—is also raised, in a way, in both narratives (though in a different way in each), to the level of "image of God," and to the level of the person and communion between persons.

The revelation, and at the same time the original discovery of the "nuptial" meaning of the body, consists in presenting man, male and female, in the whole reality and truth of his body and sex ("they were naked") and at the same time in full freedom from any constraint of the body and of sex. The nakedness of our progenitors, interiorly free from shame, seems to bear witness to this. It can be said that, created by Love, that is, endowed in their being with masculinity and femininity, they are both "naked" because they are free with the very freedom of the gift.

This freedom lies precisely at the basis of the nuptial meaning of the body: the human body, with its sex, and its masculinity and femininity, seen in the very mystery of creation, is not only a source of fruitfulness and procreation, as in the whole natural order, but includes right "from the beginning" the "nuptial" attribute, that is, *the capacity of expressing love: that love precisely in which the man-person becomes a gift* and—by means of this gift—fulfils the very meaning of his being and existence.

The root of that original nakedness free from shame, of which Genesis 1:25 speaks, must be sought precisely in that complete truth about man. Man or woman, in the context of their beatifying "beginning," are free with the very freedom of the gift. In fact, to be able to remain in the relationship of the "sincere gifts of themselves" and to become such a gift for each other through the whole of their humanity made of femininity and masculinity (also in relation to that perspective of which Gen. 2:24 speaks), they must be free precisely in this way.

We mean here freedom particularly as *mastery of oneself* (self-control). From this aspect, it is indispensable *in order that man may be able to "give himself,"* in order that he may become a gift, in order that (referring to the words of the Council) he will be able to "fully discover his true self" in "a sincere giving of himself."

The human body, oriented interiorly by the "sincere gift" of the person, reveals not only its masculinity or femininity on the physical plane, but reveals also such a value and such a beauty as to go beyond the purely physical dimension of "sexuality."[12] In this manner awareness of the nuptial meaning of the body, connected with man's masculinity-femininity, is in a way completed. On the one hand, this meaning indicates a particular capacity of expressing love, in which man becomes a gift; on the other hand, there corresponds to it the capacity and deep availability for the "affirmation of the person," that is, literally, the capacity of living the fact that the other—the woman for the man and the man for the woman—is, by means of the body, someone willed by the Creator "for his (her) own sake," that is, unique and unrepeatable: someone chosen by eternal Love.

The "affirmation of the person" is nothing but acceptance of the gift, which, by means of reciprocity, creates the communion of persons. The latter is constructed from within, comprising also the whole "exteriority" of man, that is, everything that constitutes the pure and simple nakedness of the body in its masculinity and femininity. Then—as we read in Genesis 2:25—man and woman were not ashamed. The biblical expression "were not ashamed" directly indicates "the experience" as a subjective dimension.

This "nuptial" meaning of the human body can be understood only in the context of the person. The body has a "nuptial" meaning because the man-person, as the Council says, is a creature that God willed for its own sake, and that, at the same time, can fully discover its true self only in a sincere giving of itself.

If Christ revealed to man and woman, over and above the vocation to marriage, another vocation—namely, that of renouncing marriage, in view of the kingdom of heaven—He highlighted, with this vocation, the same truth about the human person. If a man or a woman are capable of making a gift of themselves for the kingdom of heaven, this proves in its turn (and perhaps even more) that there is the freedom of the gift in the human body. It means that this body possesses a full "nuptial" meaning.

VII

Ethically Conditioned

Man enters the world and, as it were, the most intimate pattern of his future and his history, with awareness of the nuptial meaning of his own body, of his own masculinity and femininity. Original innocence says that that meaning is conditioned "ethically" and furthermore that, on its part, it constitutes the future of the human *ethos.* This is very important for the theology of the body: it is the reason why we must construct this theology "from the beginning," carefully following the indication of Christ's words.

In the mystery of creation, man and woman were "given" in a special way to each other by the Creator, and that not only in the dimension of that first human couple and of that first communion of persons, but in the whole perspective of the existence of mankind and of the human family. The fundamental fact of this existence of man at every stage of his history is that God "created them male and female"; in fact, he always creates them in this way and they are always such. Understanding of the fundamental meanings, contained in the very mystery of creation, such as the nuptial meaning of the body (and of the fundamental conditionings of this meaning), is important and indispensable in order to know who man is and who he should be, and therefore how he should mould his own activity. It is an essential and important thing for the future of the human *ethos.*

From here there begins that communion of persons, in which both meet and give themselves to each other in the fullness of their subjectivity. Thus both grow as persons-subjects, and they grow mutually one for the other also through their body and through that "nakedness" free of shame. In this communion of persons the whole depth of the original solitude of man (of the first one and of all) is perfectly ensured and, at the same time, this solitude becomes in a marvellous way permeated and broadened by the gift of the "other." If the man and the woman cease to be a disinterested gift for each other, as they were in the mystery of creation, then they recognize that "they are naked" (cf. Gen. 3). And then the shame of that nakedness, which they had not felt in the state of original innocence, will spring up in their hearts.

Original innocence manifests and at the same time constitutes the perfect *ethos* of the gift.

The Book of Genesis points out that man and woman were created for marriage: ". . . a man leaves his father and his mother and cleaves to his wife, and they become one flesh" (Gen. 2:24). In this way there opens the great creative perspective of human existence, which is always renewed by means of "procreation" which is "self-reproduction." This perspective is rooted in the consciousness of mankind and also in the particular understanding of the nuptial meaning of the body, with its masculinity and femininity. Man and woman, in the mystery of creation, are a mutual gift. Original innocence manifests and at the same time determines the perfect ethos of the gift.

We spoke about that at the preceding meeting. Through the ethos of the gift the problem of the "subjectivity" of man, who is a subject made in the image and likeness of God, is partly outlined. In the narrative of creation (particularly in Gen. 2:23–25) "the woman" is certainly not merely "an object" for the man, though they both remain in front of each other in all the fullness of their objectivity as creatures, as "bone of my bones and flesh of my flesh," as male and female, both naked. Only the nakedness that makes woman an "object" for man, or vice versa, is a source of shame. The fact that "they were not ashamed" means that the woman was not an "object" for the man nor he for her.

Interior innocence as "purity of heart," made it impossible somehow for one to be reduced by the other to the level of a mere object. The fact that they "were not ashamed" means that they were united by awareness of the gift, they were mutually conscious of the nuptial meaning of their bodies, in which the freedom of the gift is expressed and all the interior riches of the person as subject are manifested.

This mutual interpenetration of the "self" of the human persons, of the man and of the woman, seems to exclude subjectively any "reduction to an object." In this is revealed the subjective profile of that love, of which it can be said, on the other hand, that "it is objective" to the depths, since it is nourished by the mutual "objectivity" of the gift.

After original sin, man and woman will lose the grace of original innocence. The discovery of the nuptial meaning of the body will cease to be for them a simple reality of revelation and grace. However, this meaning will remain as a commitment given to man by the ethos of the gift, inscribed in the depths of the human heart, as a distant echo of original innocence. From that nuptial meaning human love in its interior truth and its subjective authenticity will be formed. And man—also through the veil of shame—will continually rediscover himself as the guardian of the mystery of the subject, that is, of the freedom of the gift, so as to defend it from any reduction to the position of a mere object.

So in man created in the image of God there was revealed, in a way, the very sacramentality of creation, the sacramentality of the world. Man, in fact, by means of his corporality, his masculinity and femininity, becomes a visible sign of the economy of Truth and Love, which has its source in God himself and which was revealed already in the mystery of creation. Against this vast background we understand fully the words that constitute the sacrament of marriage, present in Genesis 2:24 ("A man leaves his father and his mother and cleaves to his wife, and they become one flesh").

Against this vast background, we understand furthermore that the words of Genesis 2:25 ("they were both naked, and were not ashamed"), through the whole depth of their anthropological meaning, express the fact that, together with man, holiness entered the visible world, created for him. The sacrament of the world, and the sacrament of man in the world, comes from the divine source of holiness, and at the same time is instituted for holiness. Original innocence, connected with the experience of the nuptial meaning of the body, is the same holiness that enables man to express himself deeply with his own body, and that, precisely, by means of the "sincere gift" of himself. Awareness of the gift conditions, in this case, "the sacrament of the body": in his body as male or female, man feels he is a subject of holiness.

With this consciousness of the meaning of his own body, man, as male and female, enters the world as a subject of truth and love. It can be said that Genesis 2:23–25 narrates, as it were, the first feast of humanity in all the original fullness of the experience of the nuptial meaning of the body. It is a feast of humanity, which draws its origin from the divine sources of Truth and Love in the very mystery of creation. And although, very soon, the horizon of sin and death is extended over that original feast (Gen. 3), yet right from the mystery of creation we already draw a first hope: that is, that the fruit of the divine economy of truth and love, which was revealed "at the beginning" is not Death, but Life, and not so much the destruction of the body of the man created "in the image of God," as rather the "call to glory" (cf. Rom. 8:30).

1. To the ensemble of our analyses, dedicated to the biblical "beginning," we wish to add another short passage, taken from chapter 4 of the Book of Genesis. For this purpose, however, it is always necessary to refer first of all to the words spoken by Jesus Christ in the talk with the Pharisees (cf. Mt. 19 and Mk. 10), in the compass of which our reflections take place. They concern the context of human existence, according to which death and the destruction of the body connected with it (according to the words: "to dust you shall return" of Gen. 3:19) have become the common fate of man. Christ refers to "the beginning," to the original dimension of the mystery of creation, when this dimension had already been shattered by the *mysterium inquitatis*, that is, by sin and, together with it, also by death: *mysterium mortis.*

Sin and death entered man's history, in a way, through the very heart of that unity which, from "the beginning," was formed by man and woman, created and called to become "one flesh" (Gen. 2:24). Already at the beginning of our meditations we saw that Christ, referring to "the beginning," leads us in a certain way, beyond the limit of man's hereditary sinfulness to his original innocence. He enables us, in this way, to find the continuity and the connection existing between these two situations, by means of which the drama of the origins was produced as well as the revelation of the mystery of man to historical man.

This, so to speak, authorizes us to pass, after the analyses concerning the state of original innocence, to the last of them, that is, to the analysis of "knowledge and of procreation." Thematically, it is closely bound up with the blessing of fertility, which is inserted in the first narrative of man's creation as male and female (Gen. 1:27–28). Historically, on the other hand, it is already inserted in that horizon of sin and death which, as the Book of Genesis teaches (Gen. 3), has weighed on the consciousness of the meaning of the human body, together with the breaking of the first covenant with the Creator.

UNION DEFINED AS KNOWLEDGE

2. In Genesis 4, and therefore still within the scope of the Yahwist text, we read: "Adam knew Eve his wife, and she conceived and bore Cain, saying, 'I have gotten a man with the help of the Lord.' And again, she bore his brother Abel" (Gen. 4:1–2). If we connect with "knowledge" that first fact of the birth of a man on earth, we do so on the basis of the literal translation of the text, according to which the conjugal "union" is defined as "knowledge": "Adam *knew* Eve his wife," a translation of the Semitic term *yada'*.[13]

We can see in this a sign of the poverty of the archaic language, which lacked varied expressions to define differentiated facts. Nevertheless, it is significant that the situation, in which husband and wife unite so closely as to become "one flesh," has been defined as "knowledge." In this way, in fact, from the very poverty of the language there seems to emerge a specific depth of meaning, which derives, precisely, from all the meanings hitherto analysed.

BECOMING ONE

3. Evidently, this is also important as regards the "archetype" of our way of conceiving corporeal man, his masculinity and his femininity, and therefore his sex. In this way, in fact, through the term "knowledge" used in Genesis 4:1–2 and often in the Bible, the conjugal relationship of man and woman, that is, the fact that they become, through the duality of sex, "one flesh," was raised and introduced into the specific dimension of persons. Genesis 4:1–2 speaks only of "knowledge" of the woman by the man, as if to stress above all the activity of the latter. It is also possible, however, to speak of the reciprocity of this "knowledge," in which man and woman participate by means of their body and their sex. Let us add that a series of subsequent biblical texts, as, moreover, the same chapter of Genesis (cf. for example Gen. 4:17, 25), speak with the same language. And so up to the words spoken by Mary of Nazareth in the Annunciation: "How shall this be, since I know not man" (Lk. 1:34).

DEEPEST REALITY

4. Thus, with that biblical "knew," which appears for the first time in Genesis 4:1–2, we find ourselves in the presence of, on the

one hand, the direct expression of human intentionality (beause it is characteristic of knowledge) and, on the other, of the whole reality of conjugal life and union, in which man and woman become "one flesh."

Speaking here of "knowledge," even though due to the poverty of the language, the Bible indicates the deepest essence of the reality of married life. This essence appears as an element and at the same time a result of those meanings, the trace of which we have been trying to follow from the beginning of our study; it is part, in fact, of the awareness of the meaning of one's own body. In Genesis 4:1, becoming "one flesh," the man and the woman experience in a particular way the meaning of their body. Together, they become, in this way, almost the one subject of that act and that experience, while remaining in this unity, two really different subjects. In a way, this authorizes the statement that "the husband knows his wife" or that both "know" each other. They reveal themselves to each other, with that specific depth of their own human "self," which, precisely, is revealed also by means of their sex, their masculinity and femininity. And then, in a unique way, the woman "is given" to the man to be known, and he to her.

In this way, therefore, the reality of the conjugal union, in which the man and the woman become "one flesh," contains a new and, in a way, definitive discovery of the meaning of the human body in its masculinity and femininity. But, in connection with this discovery, is it right to speak only of "sexual life together"? It is necessary to take into consideration that each of them, man and woman, is not just a passive object, defined by his or her own body and sex, and in this way determined "by nature." On the contrary, precisely because of the fact that they are a man and a woman, each of them is "given" to the other as a unique and unrepeatable subject, as "self," as a person.

Sex decides not only the somatic individuality of man, but defines at the same time his personal identity and concreteness. Precisely in this personal identity and concreteness, as an unrepeatable female-male "self," man is "known" when the words of Genesis 2:24 come true: "A man . . . cleaves to his wife, and they become one flesh." The "knowledge," of which Genesis 4:1–2 and all the following biblical texts speak, arrives at the deepest roots of this identity and concreteness, which man and woman owe to their sex. This concreteness means both the uniqueness and the unrepeatability of the person.

It was worthwhile, therefore, to reflect on the eloquence of the biblical text quoted and of the word "knew." In spite of the apparent lack of terminological precision, it allows us to dwell on the depth and dimension of a concept, of which our contemporary language, very precise though it is, often deprives us.

The "man" who, according to Genesis 4:1, "knows" the woman, his wife, for the first time, in the act of conjugal union, is, in fact, that same man who, by imposing names, that is also by "knowing," "differentiated himself" from the whole world of living beings or *animalia* affirming himself as a person, and subject. The "knowledge," of which Genesis 4:1 speaks, does not and cannot take him away from the level of that original and fundamental self-awareness. So—whatever a one-sidedly "naturalistic" mentality might say about it—in Genesis 4:1 it cannot be a question of passive acceptance of one's own determination by the body and by sex, precisely because it is a question of "knowledge."

It is, on the contrary, a further discovery of the meaning of one's own body, a common and reciprocal discovery, just as the existence of man, whom "God created male and female" is common and reciprocal from the beginning. Knowledge, which was at the basis of man's original solitude, is now at the basis of this unity of the man and the woman, the clear perspective of which was enclosed by the Creator in the very mystery of creation (Gen. 1:27; 2:23). In this "knowledge," man confirms the meaning of the name "Eve," given to his wife, "because she was the mother of all living" (Gen. 3:20).

So "knowledge" in the biblical sense means that the "biological" determination of man, by his body and sex, stops being something passive, and reaches the specific level and content of self-conscious and self-determinant persons. Therefore, it involves a particular consciousness of the meaning of the human body, bound up with fatherhood and motherhood.

Although there are deep differences between man's state of original innocence and his state of hereditary sinfulness, that "image of God" constitutes a basis of continuity and unity. The "knowledge," of which Genesis 4:1 speaks, is the act which originates being, or rather, which in union with the Creator, establishes a new man in his existence. The first man, in his transcendental solitude, took possession of the visible world, created for him, knowing and imposing names on living things (*animalia*). The same "man," as male and female, knowing each other in this specific community-communion of persons, in which the man and woman are united so closely with each other as to become "one flesh," constitutes humanity, that is, confirms and renews the existence of man as the image of God. Every time both of them, man and woman, take up again, so to speak, this image from the mystery of creation, they transmit it "with the help of the Lord God."

The words of the Book of Genesis, which are a testimony of the first birth of man on earth, enclose within them at the same time everything that can and must be said of the dignity of human generation.

VIII

Need of Fulfilment of the Law

The statement to which we are now referring, that is, Matthew 5:27–28, will certainly introduce us—not only to the immediate context in which it appears—but also to its wider context, the global context, through which the key meaning of the theology of the body will be revealed to us. This statement is one of the passages of the Sermon on the Mount in which Jesus Christ makes a fundamental revision of the way of understanding and carrying out the moral law of the Old Covenant. It refers, in order, to the following commandments of the Decalogue: the fifth, "You shall not kill" (cf. Mt. 5:21–26); the sixth, "You shall not commit adultery" (cf. Mt. 5:27–32)—it is significant that at the end of this passage there also appears the question of the "certificate of divorce" (cf. Mt. 5:31–32), already mentioned in the preceding chapter—and the eighth commandment according to the text of Exodus (cf. Ex. 20:7), "You shall not swear falsely, but shall perform to the Lord what you have sworn" (cf. Mt. 5:33–37).

Significant, above all, are the words that precede these articles—and the following ones—of the Sermon on the Mount, the words in which Jesus declares: "Think not that I have come to abolish the law and the prophets, I have come not to abolish them but to fulfil them" (Mt. 5:17). In the sentences that follow, Jesus explains the meaning of this opposition and the necessity of the "fulfilment" of the Law in order to realize the kingdom of God: "Whoever . . . does them (these commandments) and teaches them shall be called great in the kingdom of heaven" (Mt. 5:19). "The kingdom of heaven" means the kingdom of God in the eschatological dimension.

The fulfilment of the Law conditions, fundamentally, this kingdom in the temporal dimension of human existence. It is a question, however, of a fulfilment that fully corresponds to the meaning of the Law, of the Decalogue, of the individual commandments. Only this fulfilment constructs that justice that God the Legislator willed. Christ the Teacher urges us not to give such a human interpretation of the whole Law and the individual commandments contained in it that it does not construct the justice willed by God the Legislator: "Unless your righteousness exceeds that of the scribes and Pharisees, you will never enter the kingdom of heaven" (Mt. 5:20).

Aspects of Fulfilment

In this context there appears Christ's statement according to Matthew 5:27–28 which we intend to take as the basis for the present analyses, considering it, together with the other statement according to Matthew 19:3–9 (and Mk. 10), as the key to the theology of the body. Like the other one, this one has an explicitly normative character. It confirms the principle of human morality contained in the commandment "you shall not commit adultery," and, at the same time, it determines an appropriate and full understanding of this principle, that is, an understanding of the foundation and at the same time of the condition for its adequate "fulfilment." The latter is to be considered precisely in the light of the words of Matthew 5:17–20, already quoted before, to which we have just drawn attention.

It is a question here, on the one hand, of adhering to the meaning that God the Legislator enclosed in the commandment "you shall not commit adultery," and, on the other hand, of carrying out that "justice" on the part of man, a justice that must "superabound" in man himself, that is, it must reach its specific fullness in him. These are, so to speak, the two aspects of "fulfilment" in the evangelical sense.

At the Heart of "Ethos"

We find ourselves in this way at the heart of *ethos*, that is, in what can be defined the interior form, almost the soul, of human morality. Contemporary thinkers (e.g., Scheler) see in the Sermon on the Mount a great turning point in the field of *ethos*.[14] A living morality, in the existential sense, is not formed only by the norms that invest the form of the commandments, precepts and prohibitions, as in the case of "you shall not commit adultery." The morality in which there is realized the very meaning of being a man—which is, at the same time, the fulfilment of the Law by means of the "super-abounding" of justice through subjective vitality—is formed in the interior perception of values, from which there springs duty as the expression of conscience, as the response of one's own personal "ego." At the same time *ethos* makes us enter the depth of the norm itself and descend within the man-subject of morality. Moral value is connected with the dynamic process of man's intimacy. To reach it, it is not enough to stop "at the surface" of human actions. It is necessary to penetrate inside.

Interior Justice

In addition to the commandment "you shall not commit adultery," the Decalogue has also "you shall not covet your neighbour's wife."[15] In the Sermon on the Mount, Christ connects them with each other, in a way: "Everyone who looks at a woman lustfully has already committed adultery with her in his heart." However, it is not a question so much of distinguishing the scope of those two commandments of the Decalogue as of pointing out the dimension of the interior action, referred to also in the words "you shall not commit adultery."

This action finds its visible expression in the "act of the body," an act in which the man and the woman participate against the law of matrimonial exclusiveness. The casuistry of the books of the Old Testament, which aimed at investigating what, according to exterior criteria, constituted this "act of the body" and was, at the same time, directed at combatting adultery, opened to the latter various legal "loopholes."[16] In this way, on the basis of the multiple compromises "for hardness of heart" (Mt. 19:8), the meaning of the commandment, willed by the Legislator, underwent a distortion. People kept to legalistic observance of the formula, which did not "superabound" in the interior justice of hearts.

Christ shifts the essence of the problem to another dimension, when he says: "Every one who looks at a woman lustfully has already committed adultery with her in his heart." (According to ancient translations: "has already made her an adulteress in his heart," a formula which seems to be more exact.)[17]

In this way, therefore, Christ appeals to the interior man. He does so several times and under different circumstances. In this case it seems particularly explicit and eloquent, not only with regard to the configuration of evangelical *ethos*, but also with regard to the way of viewing man. It is not only the ethical reason, therefore, but also the anthropological one, that makes advisable to dwell at greater length on the text of Matthew 5:27–28, which contains the words spoken by Christ in the Sermon on the Mount.

IX

The man, to whom Jesus refers here, is precisely "historical" man, the one whose "beginning" and "theological prehistory" we traced in the preceding series of analyses. Directly, it is the one who hears with his own ears the Sermon on the Mount. But together with him, there is also every other man, set before that moment of history, both in the immense space of the past, and in the equally vast one of the future. To this "future," confronted with the Sermon on the Mount, there belongs also our present, our contemporary age.

This man is, in a way, "every" man, "each" of us. Both the man of the past and also the man of the future can be the one who knows the positive commandment "you shall not commit adultery" as "contained in the Law" (cf. Rom. 2:22–23), but he can equally be the one who, according to the letter to the Romans, has this commandment only "written on his heart" (cf. Rom. 2:15).[18] In the light of the previous reflections, he is the man who from his "beginning" has acquired a precise sense of the meaning of the body, already before crossing "the threshold" of his historical experiences, in the very mystery of creation, since he emerged from it as "male and female" (Gen.1:27). He is the historical man, who, at the "beginning" of his earthly vicissitudes, found himself "inside" the knowledge of good and evil, breaking the Covenant with his Creator. He is the male-man, who "knew" (the woman) "his wife" and "knew" her several times, and "she conceived and bore" (cf. Gen. 4:1–2) according to the Creator's plan, which went back to the state of original innocence (cf. Gen. 1:28; 2:24).

Entering into His Full Image

In his Sermon on the Mount, particularly in the words of Matthew 5:27–28, Christ addresses precisely that man. He addresses the man of a given moment of history and, at the same time, all men, belonging to the same human history. He addresses, as we have already seen, the "interior" man. Christ's words have an explicit anthropological content; they concern those perennial meanings, through which an "adequate" anthropology is constituted.

These words, by means of their ethical content, simultaneously constitute such an anthropology, and demand, so to speak, that man should enter into his full image. The man who is "flesh," and who as a male remains in relationship, through his body and sex, with woman (also the expression "you shall not commit adultery" indicates this in fact), must, in the light of these words of Christ, find himself again interiorly, in his "heart."[19] The "heart" is this dimension of humanity with which the sense of the meaning of the human body, and the order of this sense, is directly linked. It is a question, here, both of the meaning which, in preceding analyses, we called "nuptial," and of that which we denominated "generative." And of what order are we treating?

Meaning of Adultery

This part of our considerations must give an answer precisely to this question—an answer that reaches not only the ethical reasons, but also the anthropological: they remain, in fact, in a mutual relationship. For the time being, preliminarily, it is necessary to establish the meaning of the text of Matthew 5:27–28, the meaning of the expressions used in it and their mutual relationship.

Adultery, to which the aforesaid commandment refers, means a breach of the unity, by means of which man and woman only as husband and wife, can unite so closely as to be "one flesh" (Gen. 2:24). Man commits adultery if he unites in this way with a woman who is not his wife. The woman likewise commits adultery if she unites in this way with a man who is not her husband. It must be deduced from this that the "adultery in the heart," committed by the man when he "looks at a woman lustfully," means a quite definite interior act. It is a question of a desire directed, in this case, by the man towards a woman who is not his wife, in order to unite with her as if she were, that is—using once more the words of Genesis 2:4—in such a way that "they become one flesh." This desire, as an interior act, is expressed by means of the sense of sight, that is, with looks, as in the case of David and Bathsheba, to use an example taken from the Bible (cf. 2 Sam. 11:2). The connection of lust with the sense of sight has been highlighted particularly in Christ's words.

Man's Interior Act

These words do not say clearly whether the woman—the object of lust—is the wife of another or whether simply she is not the wife of the man who looks at her in this way. She may be the wife of another, or even not bound by *marriage.* It is necessary rather to intuit it, on the basis particularly of the expression which, precisely, defines as adultery what man has committed "in his heart" with his look. It must be correctly deduced that this lustful look, if addressed to his own wife, is not adultery "in his heart," precisely because the man's interior act refers to the woman who is his wife, with regard to whom adultery cannot take place. If the conjugal act as an exterior act, in which "they become one flesh," is lawful in the relationship of the man in question with the woman who is his wife, in like manner also the interior act in the same relationship is in conformity with morality.

Clarifying the Text

Nevertheless, that desire, indicated by the expression "every one who looks at a woman lustfully," has a biblical and theological dimension of its own, which we cannot but clarify here. Even if this dimension is not manifested directly in this one concrete expression of Mt. 5:27–28, it is, however, deeply rooted in the global context, which refers to the revelation of the body. We must go back to this context, in order that Christ's appeal "to the heart," to the interior man, may ring out in all the fullness of its truth.

The statement of the Sermon on the Mount quoted (Mt. 5:27–28) has fundamentally an indicative character. The fact that Christ directly addresses man as the one "who looks at a woman lustfully," does not mean that his words, in their ethical meaning, do not refer also to woman. Christ expresses himself in this way to illustrate with a concrete example how "the fulfilment of the Law" must be understood, according to the meaning that God the Legislator gave to it, and furthermore how that "superabounding of justice" in the man who observes the sixth commandment of the Decalogue must be understood.

Speaking in this way, Christ wants us, not to dwell on the example in itself, but also to penetrate the full ethical and anthropological meaning of the statement. If it has an indicative character, this means that, following its traces, we can arrive at understanding the general truth about "historical" man, which is valid also for the theology of the body. The further stages of our reflections will have the purpose of bringing us closer to understanding this truth.

X

Man Alienated from Love

In all this, "nakedness" has not solely a literal meaning. It does not refer only to the body, it is not the origin of a shame related only to the body. Actually, through "nakedness," there is manifested man deprived of participation in the Gift, man alienated from that Love which had been the source of the original gift, the source of the fullness of the good intended for the creature.

This man, according to the formulas of the theological teaching of the Church,[20] was deprived of the supernatural and preternatural gifts which were part of his "endowment" before sin. Furthermore, he suffered a loss in what belongs to his nature itself, to humanity in the original fullness "of the image of God." The three forms of lust do not correspond to the fullness of that image, but precisely to the loss, the deficiencies, the limitations that appeared with sin.

Lust is explained as a lack, which, however, has its roots in the original depth of the human spirit. If we wish to study this phenomenon in its origins, that is, at the threshold of the experiences of "historical" man, we must take into consideration all the words that God Yahweh addressed to the woman (Gen. 3:16) and to the man (Gen. 3:17–19), and furthermore we must examine the state of their consciousness; and it is the Yahwist text that expressly enables us to do so. We have already called attention before to the literary specificity of the text in this connection.

A Radical Change

What state of consciousness can be manifested in the words "I was afraid, because I was naked; and I hid myself"? To what interior truth do they correspond? To what meaning of the body do they correspond? To what meaning of the body do they testify? Certainly this new state differs a great deal from the original one. The words of Genesis 3:10 bear witness directly to a radical change of the meaning of original nakedness. In the state of original innocence, nakedness, as we pointed out previously, did not express a lack, but represented full acceptance of the body in all its human and therefore personal truth.

The body, as the expression of the person, was the first sign of man's presence in the visible world. In that world, man was able, right from the beginning, to distinguish himself, almost to be individualized—that is, confirm himself as a person—also through his own body. In fact, it had been marked, so to speak, as a visible factor of the transcendence in virtue of which man, as a person, surpasses the visible world of living beings (*animalia*). In this sense, the human body was from the beginning a faithful witness and a tangible verification of man's original "solitude" in the world, becoming at the same time, by means of his masculinity and femininity, a limpid element of mutual donation in the communion of persons.

In this way, the human body bore in itself, in the mystery of creation, an unquestionable sign of the "image of God" and constituted also the specific source of the certainty of that image, present in the whole human being. Original acceptance of the body was, in a way, the basis of the acceptance of the whole visible world. And in its turn it was for man a guarantee of his dominion over the world, over the earth, which he was to subdue (cf. Gen. 1:28).

Loss of God's Image

The words "I was afraid, because I was naked; and I hid myself" (Gen. 3:10), bear witness to a radical change in this relationship. Man loses, in a way, the original certainty of the "image of God," expressed in his body. He also loses to some extent the sense of his right to participate in the perception of the world, which he enjoyed in the mystery of creation. This right had its foundation in man's inner self, in the fact that he himself participated in the divine vision of the world and of his own humanity; which gave him deep peace and joy in living the truth and value of his own body, in all its simplicity, transmitted to him by the Creator: "God saw (that) it was very good" (Gen. 1:31).

The words of Gen. 3:10: "I was afraid, because I was naked; and I hid myself," confirm the collapse of the original acceptance of the body as a sign of the person in the visible world. At the same time, the acceptance of the material world in relation to man also seems to be shaken. The words of God-Yahweh are a forewarning, in a way, of the hostility of the world, the resistance of nature with regard to man and his tasks. They are a forewarning of the fatigue that the human body was to feel in contact with the earth subdued by him: "Cursed is the ground because of you; in toil you shall eat of it all the days of your life; thorns and thistles it shall bring forth to you; and you shall eat the plants of the field. In the sweat of your face you shall eat bread till you return to the ground, for out of it you were taken" (Gen. 3:17–19). The end of this toil, of this struggle of man with the earth, is death: "You are dust, and to dust you shall return" (Gen. 3:19).

In this context, or rather in this perspective, Adam's words in Genesis 3:10: "I was afraid, because I was naked, and I hid myself," seem to express the awareness of being defenceless, and the sense of insecurity of his bodily structure before the processes of nature, operating with inevitable determinism. Perhaps, in this overwhelming statement there is implicit a certain "cosmic share," in which the being created in "the image of God" and called to subdue the earth and dominate it (cf. Gen. 1:28) expresses himself precisely when, at the beginning of his historical experiences and in a manner so explicit he is subjected to the earth, particularly in the "part" of his transcendent constitution represented precisely by the body.

NOTES

1. Creating non-living matter, God "separated"; to the animals he gave the order to be fruitful and multiply, but the difference of sex is underlined only in regard to man ("male and female he created them") by blessing at the time of their fruitfulness, that is, the bond of the persons (Gen. 1:27, 28).

2. The original text states: "God created man (*ha-'adam*—a collective noun: 'humanity'?) in his own image; in the image of God he created him; male (*zakar*—masculine) and female (*neqebah*—feminine) he created them" (Gen. 1, 27).

3. *Hace sublimis veritus:* "I am who I am" (Ex. 3, 14) constitutes an object of reflection for many philosophers, beginning from St. Augustine who held that Plato must have known this text because it seemed very close to his ideas. The Augustinian doctrine of the divine "essentialitas" has exercised, through St. Anselm, a profound influence on the theology of Richard of St. Victor, Alexander of Hales and St. Bonaventure.

   "To pass from this philosophical interpretation of Exodus to that put forward by St. Thomas, one had necessarily to bridge the gap that separated 'the being of essence' from 'the being of existence'. The Thomistic proofs of the existence of God bridged it."

   Different from this is the position of Master Eckhart, who on the basis of this text attributes to God the "puritas essendi": "est aliquid altius ente . . ." (the purity of being: he is something higher than ens) (cf. E. Gilson, *Le Thomisme,* Paris 1944 [Vrin], p. 122–127; E. Gilson, *History of Christian Philosophy in the Middle Ages,* London 1955 [Sheed and Ward], p. 810).

4. If in the language of the rationalism of the 19th century, the term "myth" indicated what was not contained in reality, the product of the imagination (Wundt), or what is irrational (Levy-Bruhl), the 20th century has modified the concept of myth.

   L. Walk sees in myth natural philosophy, primitive and areligious; R. Otto considers it as the instrument of religious knowledge; for C. G. Jung, however, myth is the manifestation of the archtypes and the expression of the "collective unconsciousness," the symbol of the interior processes.

   M. Eliade discovers in myth the structure of the reality that is inaccessible to rational and empirical investigation. Myth, in fact, transforms the event into a category, and makes us capable of perceiving the transcendental reality. It is not merely a symbol of the interior processes (as Jung states), but it is an autonomous and creative act of the human spirit, by means of which revelation is realized (cf. M. Eliade, *Traite d'histoire des religions,* Paris 1949, p. 363; *Images et symboles,* Paris 1952, pp. 199–235).

   According to P. Tillich myth is a symbol, constituted by the elements of reality to present the absolute and the transcendence of being, to which the religious act tends.

   H. Schlier emphasizes that the myth does not know historical facts and has no need of them, inasmuch as it describes man's cosmic destiny which is always identical.

   In short, the myth tends to know what is unknowable.

   According to P. Ricoeur: "The myth is something other than an explanation of the world, of its history and its destiny. It expresses in terms of the world, indeed of what is beyond the world, or of a second world, the understanding that man has of himself through relation with the fundamental and the limit of his existence . . . It expresses in an objective language the understanding that man has of his dependence in regard to what lies at the limit and the origin of his world" (P. Ricoeur, *Le conflit des interpretations*, Paris [Seuil], p. 383).

"The Adamic myth is *par excellence* the anthropological myth. Adam means Man; but not every myth of the 'primordial man' is an 'Adamic myth' which . . . alone is truly anthropological. By this three features are denoted:

—the aetiological myth relates the original of evil to an *ancestor* of present mankind, whose condition is homogeneous with ours . . .

—the aetiological myth is the most extreme attempt to separate the origin of evil from that of good. The aim of this myth is to establish firmly that evil has a radical origin, distinct from the more primitive source of the goodness of things . . . This distinction of what is radical and what is primitive is essential to the anthropological character of the Adamic myth. It is that which traces back to man the origin of evil placed in a creation which owes its absolute beginning to a creative act of God.

—the Adamic myth subordinates to the central figure of primordial man other figures which tend to displace the centre of the narrative, without however suppressing the primacy of the Adamic figure . . ."

5. As regards etymology, it is not excluded that the Hebrew term *'ish* is derived from a root which signifies "strength" (*ish* or *wsh*) whereas *'shshah* is linked to a series of Semitic terms whose meaning varies between "woman" and "wife."

The etymology proposed by the biblical text is of a popular character and serves to underline the unity of the origin of man and woman. This seems to be confirmed by the assonance of both terms.

6. "Religious language itself calls for the transposition from 'images' or rather 'symbolic modalities' to 'conceptual modalities' of expression.

"At first sight this transposition might appear to be a purely *extrinsic change*. Symbolic language seems inadequate to introduce the concept because of a reason that is peculiar to western culture. In this culture religious language has always been conditioned by another language, the philosophical, which is the conceptual language *par excellence* . . . If it is true that a religious vocabulary is understood only in a community which interprets it and according to a tradition of interpretation, it is also true that there does not exist a tradition of interpretation that is not 'mediated' by some philosophical conception.

"So the word 'God,' which in the biblical texts receives its meaning from the *convergence* of different modes of discourse (narratives, prophecies, legislative texts and wisdom literature, proverbs and hymns)—viewing this convergence both as the point of intersection and as the horizon evasive of any and every form—had to be absorbed in the conceptual space, in order to be reinterrupted in terms of the philosophical Absolute, as the first mover, first cause, *Actus Essendi*, perfect being, etc. Our concept of God pertains therefore to an onto-theology, in which there is organized the entire constellation of the key-words of theological semantics, but in a framework of meanings dictated by metaphysics" (Paul Ricoeur, *Ermeneutica biblica*, Brescia 1978 [Morcelliana], pp. 140–141; original title, *Biblical Hermeneutics*, Montana 1975).

The question, whether the metaphysical reduction really expresses the content which the symbolical and metaphorical language conceals within itself, is another matter.

7. The Hebrew term *'adam* expresses the collective concept of the human species, that is man who represents humanity (the Bible defines the individual using the expression: "son of man," *ben-'adam*). The contraposition; *'ish-'ishshah* underlines the sexual difference (as in Greek *'anergyne)*.

After the creation of the woman, the Bible text continues to call the first man *ha-'adam* (with the definite article), thus expressing his "corporate personality," since he has become "father of mankind," its progenitor and representative, just as Abraham was recognized as "father of believers" and Jacob was identified with Israel—the Chosen People.

8. Adam's sleep (in Hebrew *tardemah*) is a deep one (Latin: *sopor*), into which man falls without consciousness or dreams. The Bible has another term to define a dream: *halom*.
   Freud examines, on the other hand, the content of *dreams* (Latin: *somnium*), which, being formed with psychical elements "pushed back into the subconscious," make it possible, in his opinion, to allow the unconscious contents to emerge; the latter, he claims, are, in the last analysis, always sexual.
   This idea is, of course, quite alien to the biblical author.
   In the theology of the Yahwist author, the sleep into which God caused the first man to fall, emphasizes *the exclusivity of God's action* in the work of the creation of the woman; the man had no conscious participation in it. God uses his "rib" only to stress the common nature of man and of woman.

9. *Tardemah* (Italian "torpore," English "sleep") is the term that appears in Holy Scripture when, during sleep or immediately afterwards, extraordinary events are to happen (cf. Gen. 15:12; 1 Sam. 26:12; Is. 29:10; Job 4:13; 33:15). The Septuagint translates *tardemah* with *ekstasis* (ecstasy).
   In the Pentateuch *tardemah* appears only once more in a mysterious context: Abram, on God's command, has prepared a sacrifice of animals, driving away birds of prey from them. "As the sun was going down, a deep sleep fell on Abram; and lo, *a dread fell upon him*" (Gen. 15:12). Just then God begins to speak and concludes with him a covenant which is *the summit of the revelation* made to Abram.
   This scene is similar in a way to the one in the garden of Gethsemane. Jesus "began to be greatly distressed *and troubled* . . ." (Mk. 14:33) and found the Apostles "*sleeping for sorrow*" (Lk. 22:45).
   The biblical author admits in the first man a certain sense of privation and solitude ("it is not good that the man should be alone"; "for the man there was not found a helper fit for him"), even if not of fear. Perhaps this state brings about "a sleep caused by sorrow" or perhaps, as in Abram, by "a dread" of non-being; as on the threshold of the work of creation: "The earth was without form and void, and darkness was upon the face of the deep" Gen. 1:2).
   In any case, according to both texts in which the Pentateuch or rather the Book of Genesis speaks of the deep sleep (*tardemah*) there takes place a special divine action, that is, a "covenant" pregnant with consequences for the whole history of salvation: Adam begins mankind, Abram the Chosen People.

10. Cf. for example: M. Scheler, *Über Scham und Schamgefühl*, Halle 1914; Fr. Sawicki, *Fenomenologia wstydliwosci* (Phenomenology of shame), Krakow 1949; and also K. Wojtyla, *Miłości Odpowiedzialność*, Krakow 1962, pp. 165–185 (in Italian: *Amore e responsabilità*, Rome 1978, 2nd ed., pp. 161–178).

11. The concept of an "adequate anthropology" has been explained in the text itself as "understanding and interpretation of man in what is essentially human." This concept determines the very principle of reduction, characteristic of the philosophy of man, indicates the limit of this principle, and indirectly excludes the possibility of going beyond this limit. An "adequate" anthropology rests on essentially "human" experience, opposed to the reductionism of the "naturalistic" type, which often goes hand in hand with the evolutionistic theory about the beginnings of man.

12. "Furthermore, the Lord Jesus, when praying to the Father 'that they may all be one . . . even as we are one' (Jn. 17:21–22), has opened up new horizons closed to human reason by implying that there is a certain parallel between the union existing among the divine persons and the union of the sons of God in truth and love. It follows, then, that if man is the only creature on earth that God has willed for its own sake, man can fully discover his true self only in a sincere giving of himself" (GS 24).
   The strictly theological analysis of the Book of Genesis, in particular Gen. 2:23–25, allows us to refer to this text. This constitutes another step between "adequate anthro-

pology" and "theology of the body," which is closely bound up with the discovery of the essential characteristics of personal existence in man's "theological prehistory." Although this may meet with opposition on the part of the evolutionist mentality (even among theologians), it would be difficult, however, not to realize that the text of the Book of Genesis that we have analysed, especially Gen. 2:23–25, proves not only the "original," but also the "exemplary" dimension of the existence of man, in particular of man "as male and female."

13. As for archetypes, C. G. Jung describes them as "a priori" forms of various functions of the soul: perception of relations, creative fantasy. The forms fill up with content with materials of experience. They are not inert, but are charged with sentiment and tendency (see particularly: "Die psychologischen Aspekte des Mutterarchetypus," *Eranos* 6, 1938, pp. 405–409).

According to this conception, an archetype can be met within the mutual man-woman relationship, a relationship which is based on the dual and complementary realization of the human being in two sexes. The archetype will fill up with content by means of individual and collective experience, and can trigger off fantasy, the creator of images. It would be necessary to specify that the archetype: a) is not limited to, or exalted in, physical intercourse, but includes the relationship of "knowing"; b) it is charged with tendency: desire-fear, gift-possession; c) the archetype, as proto-image ("Urbild") is a generator of images ("Bilder").

The third aspect enables us to pass to hermeneutics, in the concrete, that of texts of Scripture and of Tradition. Primary religious language is symbolic (cf. W. Stahlin, *Symbolon*, 1958; J. Macquarrie, *God Talk*, 1968; T. Fawcett, *The Symbolic Language of Religion*, 1970). Among the symbols, Jung prefers some radical or exemplary ones, which we can call archetypal. Well, among them the Bible uses the symbol of the conjugal relationship, concretely at the level of the "knowing" described.

One of the first poems of the Bible, which applies the conjugal archetype to God's relations with his people, culminates in the verb commented on: "You shall know the Lord" (Hos. 2:22: *w^{e}yada'at 'et YHWH;* weakened to "You will know that I am the Lord" = *w^{e}yada'at ki 'ani YHWH:* Is. 49:23; 60:16; Ez. 16:62, which are the three "conjugal" poems). A literary tradition starts from here, which will culminate in the Pauline application of Eph. 5 to Christ and to the Church; then it will pass to patristic tradition and to that of the great mystics (for example "Llama de amor viva" of St. John of the Cross).

In the treatise *Grundzüge der Literatur- und Sprachwissenschaft*, Vol. I, Munich 1976, 4 cd., p. 462, archetypes are defined as follows: "Archaic images and motifs which, according to Jung, form the content of the collective unconscious common to all men: they present symbols, which, in all times and among all peoples, bring to life in a figurative way what is decisive for humanity as regards ideas, representations and instincts."

Freud, it seems, does not use the concept of archetype. He establishes a symbolism or code of fixed correspondences between present patent images and latent thoughts. The meaning of the symbols is fixed, even if not just one: they may be reducible to an ultimate thought that is irreducible, which is usually some experience of childhood. These are primary and of sexual character (but he does not call them archetypes). See T. Todorov, *Theories du symbole*, Paris 1977, pp. 317 f.; also: J. Jacoby, *Komplex, Archetyp, Symbol in der Psychologie C. G. Jungs*, Zurich 1957.

14. "Ich kenne kein grandiöseres Zeugnis für eine solche Neuerschliessung eines ganzen Wertbereiches, die das ältere Ethos relativiert, als die Bergpredigt, die auch in ihrer Form als Zeugnis solcher Neuerschliessung und Relativierung der älteren 'Gesetzeswerte' sich überall kundgibt: 'Ich aber sage euch' " (Max Scheler, *Der Formalismus in der Ethik und die materiale Wertethik*, Halle 1921, p. 310, n. 1).

15. Cf. Ex. 20:17; Dt. 5:21.

16. On this point, see the continuation of the present meditations.

17. The text of the Vulgate offers a faithful translation of the original: *iam moechatus est cum in corde suo.* In fact, the Greek verb *moichcuo* is transitive. In modern European languages, on the other hand, "to commit adultery" is an intransitive verb; so we get the translation: "has committed adultery with her." And thus, ". . . *has already committed adultery with her in his heart*" (Douai Version, 1582; similarly Revised Standard Version from 1611 to 1966, R. Knox, New English Bible, Jerusalem Bible, 1966).

18. In this way, the content of our reflections shifts, in a way, to the field of "natural law." The words quoted from the Letter to the Romans (2:15) have always been considered, in revelation, as a source of confirmation for the existence of natural law. Thus the concept of natural law also acquires a theological meaning.

Cf. among others, D. Composta, *Teologia del diritto naturale, status quaestionis,* Brescia 1972 (Fd. Civilta), pp. 7–22, 41–53; J. Fuchs S. J., *Lex naturae. Zur Theologie des Naturrechts,* Düsseldorf 1955, pp. 22–30; E. Hamel S. J. *Loi naturelle et loi du Christ.* Bruges-Paris 1964 (Desclee de Brouwer) p. 18; A. Sacchi, "La legge naturale nella Bibbia" in: *La legge naturale. Le relazioni del Convegno dei teologi moralisti dell'Italia settentriontale* (11–13 September 1969), Bologna 1970 (Ed. Dehoniane), p. 53; F. Bockle, "La legge naturale e la legge cristiana," *ibid.,* pp. 214–215; A. Feuillet, "Le fondement de la morale ancienne et chretienne d'apres l'Epitre aux Romains," *Revue Thomiste* 78 (1970) 357–386; Th. Herr, *Naturrecht aus der kritischen Sicht des Neuen Testaments,* Munich 1976 (Schöning), pp. 155–164.

19. "The typically Hebraic usage reflected in the New Testament implies an understanding of man as unity of thought, will and feeling. (. . .) It depicts man as a whole, viewed from his intentionality; *the heart as the center* of man is thought of as source of will, emotion, thoughts and affections.

"This traditional Judaic conception was related by Paul to Hellenistic categories, such as 'mind,' 'attitude,' 'thoughts' and 'desires.' Such a co-ordination between Judaic and Hellenistic categories is found in Ph. 1:7; 4:7; Rom. 1:21–24, where 'heart' is thought of as the center from which these things flow" (R. Jewett, *Paul's Anthropological Terms. A Study of their Use in Conflict Settings,* Leiden 1971 [Brill], p. 448).

20. The magisterium of the Church deals more closely with these problems, in three periods, according to the needs of the age.

The declarations of the period of the controversies with the Pelagians (5th–6th centuries) affirm that the first man, by virtue of divine grace, possessed "*naturalem possibilitem et innocentiam*" (DS 239), also called "freedom" ("libertas," "libertas arbitrii"—DS 371, 242, 383, 622). He remained in a state which the Synod of Orange (in the year 529) called "integritas": "*Natura humana, etianisi in illa integritate, in qua condita est, permaneret, nulla moda se ipsam. Creatore suo non adruvante, servaret . . .*" (DS 389).

The concepts of "integritas" and, in particular, that of "libertas" presuppose freedom from concupiscence, although the ecclesiastical documents of this age do not mention it explicitly.

The first man was furthermore free from the necessity of death (DS 222, 372, 1511).

The Council of Trent defines the state of the first man, prior to sin, as "holiness and justice" ("sanctitas et iustitia"—DS 1511, 1512) or as "innocence" ("innocentia"—DS 1521).

Further declarations on this matter defend the absolute gratuitousness of the original gift of grace, against the affirmations of the Jansenists. The "integritas primae creationis" was an unmerited elevation of human nature ("indebita humanae naturae exaltatio") and not "the state due to him by nature" ("naturalis eius condicio"—DS 1926). God, therefore, could have created man without these graces and gifts (DS 1955), that would not have shattered the essence of human nature and would not have deprived it of its fundamental privileges (DS 1903–1907, 1909, 1921, 1923, 1924, 1926, 1935, 2434, 2437, 2616, 2617).

In analogy with the anti-Pelagian Synods, the Council of Trent deals above all with the dogma of original sin, integrating in its teaching preceding declarations in this connection. Here however, a certain clarification was introduced, which partly changed the content comprised in the concept of "liberum arbitrium." The "freedom" or "free will" of the anti-Pelagian documents did not mean the possibility of choice, connected with human nature, and therefore constant, but referred only to the possibility of carrying out meritorious acts, the freedom that springs from grace and that man may lose.

Well, because of sin, Adam lost what did not belong to human nature in the strict sense of the word, that is, "integritas," "sanctitas," "innocentia," "justitia." "Liberum arbitrium," free will, was not taken away, but became weaker:

"... liberum arbitrium minime exstinctum ... veribus licet attenuatum et inclinatum ..." (DS 1521—Trid. Sess. VI, Decr. de Justificatione, C.1).

Together with sin appears concupiscence and the inevitability of death:

"... primum hominem ... cum mandatum Dei ... fuisset transgressus, statim sanctitatem et justitiam, in qua costitutus fuerat, amisisse *incurrisseque* per offensam praevaricationis huiusmodi iram et indignationem Dei atque ideo *mortem* ... 'totumque Adam per illam praevaricationis offensam secundum corpus et aninam in deterius commutatum fuisse ...' " (DS 1511, Trid. Sess. V. Decr. de pecc. orig. 1).

(Cf. *Mysterium Salutis*, 11, Einsiedeln-Zürich-Köln 1967, pp. 827–828: W. Seibel, "Der Mensch als Gottes übernatürliches Ebenbild und der Urstand des Menschen").

4

A Christian Humanism: Sign of Contradiction

Blessèd sister, holy mother, spirit
of the fountain, spirit of the garden,
Suffer us not to mock ourselves with falsehood
Teach us to care and not to care
Teach us to sit still
Even among these rocks,
Our peace in His will . . .

T. S. ELIOT: *Ash Wednesday*

PHILOSOPHERS prior to John Paul II have diagnosed the ills from which modern man suffers. Those who stood at the bier of the last century and at the cradle of ours have described and cataloged and categorized all the symptoms.

They were there to see the spirit that made us humans leave the body and to see us transformed into machines by the materialistic systems we serve. They took note of our anxiety and loneliness, our capacity for violence and self-destruction, our estrangement from one another and, worst of all, from our own self.

"We live in a period of atomic chaos," Nietzsche wrote of the age of collectivism that was to come. That age is now. Man has let it come about, submitting to unspeakable indignities in the process and blindly surrendering his fate to those least likely to honor his trust.

But to John Paul II, man's "sickness unto death" is not incurable. In these selections, taken from a series of twenty-two spiritual exercises presented to Pope Paul VI, the papal household, and the members of the Curia at the Lenten Retreat in March 1976, John Paul II spoke of the alternative world, the ground where God and man can meet—in this day and age which appears to turn a deaf ear to God and the realm of the spirit.

From *Sign of Contradiction*

The theology of the death of God reflects a tragic crisis in present-day thought, even though in one way the thinkers of today can take genuine pride in the enormous advances that have been made in knowledge of the world . . . particularly in the field of the application of science and technology. But now, at a time when man has "subdued the earth" (Gen. 1:28; Ps. 8:6–9) to a degree never before known . . . , when he has extended so far the "horizontal" thread of his knowledge, what strikes one most forcibly is a lack of balance in relation to the "vertical" component of that knowledge. Present-day man—one could say—does not think things through to the end, does not seek the fundamental reasons why, looks for no foothold in knowledge of Him whom the Book of Wisdom proclaims as the Creator.

The modern mind, thanks to Christianity, is free of the temptation to deify the forces of nature. But, at the same time, philosophical and theoretical materialism—and everyday materialism, too—are doing their best to turn matter into an absolute in human thought. I can remember several publications, typical of the early postwar years in Poland, in which Catholic intellectuals in argument with Marxists demonstrated that matter cannot have the character of an absolute. Arguments of this type have now died down: Attention is now concentrated on the anthropological problem, although the *Weltanschauung* and the Marxist system go on asserting that matter constitutes the be-all and end-all of man, his beginning and his end, the fulness of the reality that completely defines the purpose of his existence as an individual.

What impression does the truth of God leave on the mind of the ordinary man, the nonphilosopher? It is characteristic of this fundamental truth that it survives even in conditions of systematic and planned denial of God. I shall never forget the impression left with me by a Russian soldier in 1945. The war was only just over. A conscript knocked at the door of the Cracow seminary. When I asked "what is it you want?" he replied he wished to enter the seminary. . . . Even though he never in fact did enter, our meeting taught me one great truth. . . . In the whole of his adult life that man had scarcely ever gone inside a church. At school, and then later at work, he had continually heard people asserting "There is no God!" And in spite of all that, he said more than once: "But I always knew that God exists . . . and now I would like to learn something about Him."

The concept of infinity is not unknown to man. He makes use of it in his scientific work, in mathematics, for instance. So there certainly is room in him, in his intellectual understanding, for Him who is infinite, the God of boundless majesty. . . . This God is professed in his silence by the Trappist or the Carmelite. It is to Him that the desert Bedouin turns at his hour for prayer, and perhaps the Buddhist, too, wrapt in contemplating as he purifies his thought, preparing the way to Nirvana. This is God in His absolute transcendence, God who transcends absolutely the whole of creation, all that is visible and comprehensible.

Throughout . . . Genesis, the heart can be heard beating. We have before us not a great builder of the world, a demiurge: We stand in the presence of the great heart! No cosmogony, no philosophical cosmology of the past, no cosmological theory of the present-day can express a truth like this truth. We can find it only in the inspired pages of Genesis: revelation of the love that pervades the whole earth to its very core, revelation of the Fatherhood that gives creation its full meaning, together with the covenant that gives rise to the creation of man in the image of God.

Satan, the evil spirit, is portrayed in Genesis as an already existing reality, already operating in the world. The biblical description of the creation of the universe is concerned only with visible reality, with the *earth* and the *heavens,* components of the empirical cosmos; that description is silent concerning what is a nonempirical reality. All the same, even though Genesis does not explain the origins of Satan, the evil spirit, we can at once identify him with ease when he first puts in an appearance. . . . The evil spirit is recognizable and identifiable not by means of some definition of his being but solely from the content of his words. Here, in the third chapter of Genesis, at the very beginning of the bible, it becomes clear that the history of mankind, and with it the history of the world with which man is united through the work of divine creation, will both be subject to rule by the Word and the Anti-Word, the Gospel and the Anti-Gospel. . . . When the Devil says in the third chapter of Genesis, "your eyes would open and you would become like God," these words express the full range of temptation of mankind, from the intention to set man against God to the extreme form it takes today. We could even say that in the first stage of human history this temptation not only was not accepted but had not been fully formulated. But the time has now come: This aspect of the Devil's temptation has found the historical context that suits it. Perhaps we are experiencing the highest level of tension between the Word and the Anti-Word in the whole of human history. Alienation thought of in that way implies not only denial of the God of the covenant but also of the very idea of God: denial of His existence.

The third chapter of Genesis, in which Satan first appeared on the world horizon bringing sin, also includes the first proclamation of the coming of the Savior, the Word incarnate, the Son. The proclamation . . . is a divine riposte to the first appearance . . . of the Anti-Word and the man of sin. . . . From the moment of the very first denial, truth—the divine truth—will always seek, in ways known only to itself, to penetrate world history, to enter the minds and hearts of men. The father of lies will never cease to deny it. But . . . the great heart that opened in the first chapters of Genesis does not withdraw and close again when faced with the lie, but sheds over the whole of human history, in every age including our own, the light of boundless hope.

Christ's entry into the world reveals an economy altogether *sui generis,* proper to God alone. It is a divine economy, with its source in the Father, the Son, and the Holy Spirit. From this source gush the waters of the great river that extends over the entire surface of the earth and permeates the whole of history. . . . The power that never deserted Jesus as He went about His teaching has nothing in common with the motives characteristic of human reasoning. . . . The world sorely needed a criterion of power that would be radically "other," a manifestation of a different hierarchy of values, in order that the men of that day and the men of today . . . might come to believe in the truth of love. . . . "I don't believe in love," disillusioned youngsters will sometimes say. To say "I don't believe in love" is also the natural reaction of every man who is oppressed by evil or—worse still—caught in the toils of consumerism and a prey to the hunger for status symbols that divides both the world and the hearts of men. Jesus the Christ had to enter the world in the way He did, had to pass through and out of it in the way He did, in order that the whole of His passing . . . from start to finish might confirm the truth of love.

The concentration camps will always remain in men's minds as real-life symbols of hell-on-earth; they expressed to the highest degree the evil man is capable of inflicting on his fellow men. In one such camp, Fr. Maximilian Kolbe died in 1941. All the prisoners knew that he died of his own free choice, offering his own life in exchange for that of a fellow prisoner. And with that particular revelation there passed through that hell-on-earth a breath of fearless and indestructible goodness, a kind of intimation of salvation. One man died, but humanity was saved! So close is the tie between love and salvation.

Love, an uncreated gift, is part of the inner mystery of God and is the very nucleus of theology. In creation and in the covenant love is made manifest not only as motive but also as fact, as reality, a consequence of divine working. Precisely for this reason, the world that emerged from the hands of God the Creator is itself structured on a basis of love. . . . The new and definitive covenant will restore forever to the world and to mankind the sense of receiving as a gift everything there is: every created being, every material good, all the treasures of the heart and mind; and first and foremost, the sense of receiving as a gift one's humanity, one's dignity as a human being and one's dignity as an adopted child of God Himself. . . . This is a "gift from on high," the Holy Spirit restored to mankind—to human relationships, to marriage, to the family, to the various social groupings, to nations, and to states—the fundamental sense of gift and of being "bestowed." This kind of awareness is a fruit of the spirit of Christ. . . . With this principle as a basis, it will be possible, patiently but also effectively, to overcome all that has engendered and still does engender the anti-love that St. Augustine described . . . in the formula: "*amor sui usque ad contemptum Dei.*" This "*amor sui usque ad contemptum Dei,*" in its various forms and dimensions, lies at the root of all the ruthless exploitation of men by other men: exploitation in industrial production and consumerism, exploitation by the state in the various totalitarian or crypto-totalitarian systems that start off by issuing strongly humanistic declarations but end up by violating the most elementary of human rights.

Finally, it is again the "*amor sui usque ad contemptum Dei*" that divides society into warring classes, that puts armaments in the hands of whole nations to enable them to fight one another and even engage in civil wars, and that divides the earth into so-called "worlds," which know only how to do battle with one another. . . . This anti-love, which entered the history of man and of creation, can be countered and overcome—as St. Augustine teaches us—only by love, boundless love, that is to say, "*amor Dei usque ad contemptum sui!*" . . . The love that Jesus speaks of in His farewell discourse has the dimension of the sacrifice that He Himself is about to make, so it has an historical dimension that speaks to man with all the majesty of the cross. Yet, at the same time, love has a supra-historical dimension that goes beyond history, the dimension of a gift refused by the "*amor sui usque ad contemptum Dei*" of Satan, and very often distorted or destroyed in the hearts and the history of mankind. This gift must therefore return, by way of Jesus, to its source, so that man may rediscover himself within the covenant in all its fullness. This is the "why" of the cross.

When Jesus talked with the Father in the garden of olives, He had become conscious of the full extent of His all-important duty, the duty He had already spoken of to His mother when He was twelve. But one might also say that in this conversation with the Father it is possible to perceive an expression of His indebtedness to His mother, the duty He owed to her. For it is as a true son of man that Jesus talks with the Father. He expresses all the psychological truth of His human nature, which shudders at the prospect of suffering and death. . . . His suffering extended over the whole range of human sensitivity inherited from His mother. . . . He suffered therefore in all the mystery of His person, in all the indescribable depth of His nature as God-man, the one and only subject and the one and only author of redemption of the world. He respected His mother's rights to the very end: Indeed, He drew her into the ambit of the mystery of redemption, close to His own divine-human nature. . . . Jesus Christ—true God and true man—knew He could rely on His mother as He pursued His mission. . . . He was sure of her heart, that heart which helped Him to express in human fashion, in terms of human thoughts and feelings, the great heart of the Father. This motherly heart did not fail Him at the testing time of Gethsemane and Calvary. It was close to Him on the road from Pilate's *praetorium* to Mount Calvary as He carried His cross, and it was close to Him when He drew His last breath.

The mystery of redemption infinitely surpasses the thoughts and the ways of men. It is a divine mystery in which God expresses His own self—His justice and mercy, His holiness which is love. . . . It springs from the conflict between the Word and the Anti-Word, between love and anti-love. . . . This mystery of salvation, flowing as it does from the heart and the sacrifice of the divine man of history, takes shape in an historical event; but although it occurs in time, in its inner meaning it transcends time and reaches a dimension that is divine and at the same time human. . . . The Word speaks the truth about God, who is Father and Love; working with God, it instills love. This truth and this love find expression in the obedience of Jesus, His "obedience unto death." This was the transcendental response to the disobedience of mankind, in which the "father of lies" played a part together with the anti-love generated by the lies. The Son's obedience to the Father also does justice to the God of infinite majesty, who at the same time is the God of the covenant.

From the very dawn of history, injustice has made itself at home in the world: Men, communities, nations have all treated one another unjustly. . . . Today, the world echoes with a desperate cry for social justice, for justice as it affects every man. . . . It is becoming ever more clear that the achievement of a just society, a just world, is a task that confronts every man in every age. . . . Jesus the Christ went forward toward death in full awareness of His messianic destiny. He knew that the destiny of all humanity and the whole world lay with Him and His cross. . . . On the day of His death, Jesus entered into the fullest and deepest communion and solidarity with the entire human family, especially with all those who throughout history have been the victims of injustice, cruelty, and scornful abuse. . . .

The cross was an instrument of torture for the condemned man. The cross was a chosen sign. In it, the vertical and the horizontal meet; it is thus an expression of the most profound interaction of the divine and the human. It is at this point of intersection, symbolic but also real, that we find the sacrificial lamb of God, the God-man. Jesus embraced all things in order to restore all things to His Father. And by this act of restitution, this act of sacrifice, He has made all things "new." . . . All men, from the beginning of the world until its end, have been redeemed by Christ and His cross.

Christ's presence in the Church—His eucharistic, sacramental, and at the same time charismatic presence—shows that His "going away" in death is the immediate cause of His "coming back" in the dimension of the gift, the uncreated everlasting gift, which is none other than the Holy Spirit. . . . It is a gift that expresses love, not only the love of the lamb of God on the cross . . . but also the love of the bridegroom, for whom the Church—and also every human soul "in Christ"—becomes a bride. Consequently, the Church takes shape in a new dimension: "in Christ." . . . So the love of Christ-the-bridegroom directly stems from the cross and the sacrifice. The redeemer is the bridegroom by virtue of being the redeemer! He is able to bring His gift to the Church precisely because He has already given Himself in the sacrifice of His blood. . . .

There does seem to be a need to recall and repeat to the men of our day: The bridegroom is with you! His love for you is so great that He gave Himself fully and irrevocably. Jesus wished us to inherit from Him nothing less than love of every single human being. It may seem a poor inheritance, but in fact its potential is immense. For what else does man seek except to be loved? What else gives human existence its fundamental meaning? We are poor, but we are rich. The bridegroom is with you!

Who is Jesus Christ for all the different continents of the world, for all the different societies, traditions, cultures, political situations? Jesus is the symbol of liberation from unjust structures, both social and economic, but He is also the sign of liberation for people who are denied freedom of conscience and religious freedom, or who have those freedoms drastically curtailed at crucial points. He is in every way a reproach to affluent, acquisitive consumer societies. . . . He is the touchstone of identity for the African nations that are moving toward independence. He is a Word of divine wisdom for the ancient spiritual traditions and cultures of the East.

Christ, the great prophet, is the one who proclaims divine truth; and He is also the one who shows the dignity of man to be bound up with truth: with truth honestly sought, earnestly pondered, joyfully accepted as the greatest treasure of the human spirit, witnessed to by word and deed in the sight of men. Truth has a divine dimension; it belongs by nature to God Himself; it is one with the divine Word. At the same time, it constitutes an essential dimension of human knowledge and human existence, of science, wisdom, and the human conscience. Every man is born into the world to bear witness to the truth according to his own particular vocation. . . . Man's right to the truth must never be denied. In our complex present-day world, this denial can take different forms. One form it takes is that of "manipulation" of the truth—for instance, the dissemination of some types of information and the suppression of others, the use of the mass media to pander to the cult of sensationalism typical of our times. Given these structures of present-day civilization, given the pressures they exert, each and every man's personal responsibility inevitably becomes greater because the threat to the truth constantly becomes greater. . . . Given our society today, in which falsity and hypocrisy reign supreme, public opinion is manipulated, consciences are bludgeoned, apostasy is sometimes imposed by force, and there is organized persecution of the faith. . . . The Christ who bore witness to the truth is more than ever the Christ for us. . . . Jesus of Nazareth, like all who bear witness to the truth, became a sign of contradiction for those to whom He had been sent. The signs, the miracles He performed, . . . could not get the better of that fundamental contradiction which, humanly speaking, proved stronger than He was. Jesus sealed His witness with His own blood. And this is the inheritance He has bequeathed to the Church.

By its very nature, priesthood is a reply to the insistent, profound, fundamental questions asked by man, asked by the whole *human family* about the meaning of the created world, the meaning of the whole of reality in which man belongs existentially and yet which he surpasses. The priest, simply by being who he is, expresses this meaning and at the same time conveys it to the world and to man in the world. He expresses it not by elaborating a set of arbitrary ideas but by embracing the truth, as truth's *prophet and servant*. . . . The priesthood . . . is the form of self-expression of the man for whom the world's ultimate meaning can be found only in the dimension of the transcendental: in turning toward God who, as the fullness of personal being, in Himself transcends the world. Without relationship and without self-giving, the whole of human existence on earth loses its meaning. . . . The scaffolding has been erected for the "new world," programed as a world "without God." . . . New towns are being built . . . but no churches. . . . But when this does happen, these men and women—not mainly we priests and bishops but the laity themselves— . . . will demand a church in the name of their rights as citizens, but above all . . . in the name of that fundamental truth about the world and mankind that is contained in Christ, in priesthood, in the human temple of God. Without a church, no district in this "new world" will ever discover its own true meaning; nor will it ever be fully *human.*

All human work, and all that is produced in any field of endeavor, shapes the human personality; but it does so not because of the objective value of what it produces but because of its own moral worth—a distinctively human and personal element in all man's activity, man's *praxis.* . . . The dignity of the human person has its foundation in the conscience, in that inner obedience to the objective principle that enables human praxis to distinguish between good and evil. The conscience warns against evil and urges man toward the good. It wants man to become firmly attached to what is good, not just for the time being but more profoundly; it wants him not to lose that underlying good that is his human nature itself. Man's obedience to his conscience is the key to his moral grandeur and the basis of his *kingliness,* his *dominion;* and this—ethically speaking—is also a dominion over himself.

Prayer is always a wonderful reduction of eternity to the dimension of a moment in time, a reduction of the eternal wisdom to the dimension of human knowledge, feeling, and understanding, a reduction of the eternal love to the dimension of the human heart, which at times is incapable of absorbing its riches and seems to break. . . . All prayer is a meeting between the human will and the will of God; for this we are indebted to the Son's obedience to the Father: "Your will be done." And obedience does not mean only renunciation of one's own will; it means opening one's spiritual eyes and ears to the love that is God Himself.

The course of history—in our own day especially, perhaps—shows an ever greater contrast between man's enormous material gains and his moral shortcomings, his falling short in the sphere of what he is. One can quite safely say that in the sphere of what he is man fails to match what he possesses.

Present-day personalistic philosophy seeks to emphasize the personal sense of death and dying. Even though a man does not choose his own death, nonetheless, by choosing his own way of life, he does, in a sense, choose his own way of death too. Thus, his death becomes the perfect ratification of his life and of the choice he has made.

Sin in all its theological reality, its effect on man's relationship with God, is inescapably a fact of human life; and it causes man to fall short in his treatment of himself, of others, and of the world. The whole of this *temporal* dimension of sin, linked with creation and with time, is reflected in the wonderful revealed teaching about man's purification from sin. . . . Inner purification, rightly called moral, comes by way of suffering. . . . Part of the law of suffering . . . is that it entails loneliness for man. . . . The limits of human endurance are not reached in every illness; but the closer the suffering gets to those limits, the more the sufferer has to endure it alone. That loneliness can be seen in the story of the just man Job. And when loneliness becomes the occasion for man to meet God, the purifying dimension of suffering is seen to extend beyond the confines of this life. . . . The law of purification and the reality of purgatory certainly have a profound objective meaning from which their subjective meaning stems. Both arise out of the need for man to be spirit-ually prepared for union with the living God in charity. In one sense, this union expresses the degree of purity attainable by the created human spirit. . . . The mystery of purgatory is explained not only by the order of justice and the need for expiation through temporal punishment but also—and perhaps primarily—by the order of charity and union with God. Man needs this mystery for his interior life, for his ascesis, for his steady approach toward the living God in the darkness of faith; although the darkness hides the face of the living God, it unveils the infinite majesty of His holiness.

An understanding of eschatology from man's angle alone, taking into account only man's desires and aspirations, is insufficient as a basis for proper understanding of the so-called "last things." The right basis is the plan of salvation revealed by God; and this plan, according to the logic of revelation, is that of the consummation of all things in Christ. . . . The blood of Christ's cross marks the beginning of all that mysterious and essentially divine work of salvation, justification, and sanctification that is already shaping in outline the final consummation that is to come. . . . The Son will hand all things back to the Father in the Holy Spirit. And this is what will make the consummation the "*perfectum opus laudis.*" The glory of God is the prime norm of the whole of reality, and the consummation of all things will depend on the degree to which God's glory has been made manifest. Glory is the irradiation of the good, the reflecting of all perfection. And, in one way it is also the inner atmosphere of the deity, the godhead. God lives in glory and transfuses this glory in all that He does. All His works are full of His glory: creation, redemption, sanctification, consummation. In a very special way, God transmits this glory to man. The glory of God is living man; the glory of God is man alive.

The times in which we are living provide particularly strong confirmation of the truth of what Simeon said: Jesus is both the light that shines for mankind and at the same time a sign of contradiction. . . . The great poverty of many, first and foremost the poverty of the Third World, hunger, economic exploitation, colonialism—which is not confined to the Third World—all this is a form of opposition to Christ on the part of the powerful, irrespective of political regimes and cultural traditions. This form of contradiction of Christ often goes hand-in-hand with a partial acceptance of religion, of Christianity and the Church, an acceptance of Christ as an element present in culture, morality, and even education. . . . One need only pay heed to what is passed over in silence and what is shouted aloud, one need only lend an ear to what encounters most opposition, to perceive that even where Christ is accepted there is at the same time opposition to the full truth of His person, His mission, and His Gospel. There is a desire to "reshape" Him, to adapt Him to suit mankind in this era of progress and make Him fit in with the program of modern civilization—which is a program of consumerism and not of transcendental ends. . . . This opposition to Christ, which goes hand-in-hand with paying Him lip service—and it is also to be found among those who call themselves His disciples—is particularly symptomatic of our times.

In periods when Christ, and therefore His Church, Pope, bishops, priests, religious, and all the faithful become the sign that provokes the most implacable and premeditated contradiction, Mary appears particularly close to the Church, because the Church is always in a way her Christ, first the Christ-child and then the crucified and risen Christ. If in such periods, such times in history, there arises a particular need to entrust oneself to Mary, this need flows directly from the integral logic of the faith, from rediscovery of the whole divine economy, and from understanding of its mysteries. The Father in heaven demonstrated the greatest trust in mankind by giving mankind His Son. The human creature to whom He first entrusted Him was Mary. And until the end of time, she will remain the one to whom God entrusts the whole of His mystery of salvation. . . . All that goes to make up what He bequeathed—the work of salvation, the mystical body of Christ, the people of God, the Church—is taken care of, and always will be taken care of, by her—with the same fidelity and strength that she showed in taking care of her son.

5

The Dignity of Man: Redemptor Hominis

We are a generation of men so estranged
from the inner world that many are arguing
that it does not exist
and that even if it does exist,
it doesn't matter.

R. D. LAING: *The Politics of Experience*

NOT *since the time of Pius IX's (1846–1878), proclamation of the dogma of the Immaculate Conception (1854) and the dogma of Papal Infallibility (1870) has there been a document more eagerly awaited than the first official pronouncement of the first non-Italian Pope. John Paul II issued his encyclical* Redemptor Hominis *on March 19, 1979, just four months after his election to the throne of St. Peter. In this lengthy document, John Paul confirms the moral and spiritual power of the Latin Church, its traditions, its role, and the work he proposes the Church perform in its service to Christ.*

The encyclical is largely a theological document, yet its theology is heavily mixed with politics and polemics. John Paul has announced to the world that he will not be a "quiet Pope" or a "smiling Pope" but a strong leader. No political label will contain him or explain him; no system will bind him except the one that he freely submits to. In this encyclical John Paul very clearly states that his pontificate will be devoted entirely to the basic mission of the Roman Catholic Church, to continue Christ's work as the Redeemer, to redeem man from the conditions man himself has created.

This work must be universal and unrelenting. Man has to learn how to face himself, how to understand the self that he is, and that he can be naked without feeling shame. The consciousness of being a self and of being the supreme value on earth is the only clothing the spirit of man needs.

The reality towards which John Paul II wants us to climb is contained in the commandment to love; all else is illusion. Its common name is materialism. Its symptoms are subject to cultural and ideological variations. The cure is found in the conscious awareness that man and woman are made in the image of God. The "Theology of the Body" is John Paul's first lesson in the liberation of consciousness. More such lessons are sure to come during the remainder of his pontificate, and the teacher promises to be stern.

All of this is foreshadowed in the encyclical from which we have selected those passages concerning the dignity of man, the freedom of the individual, and the growth of consciousness that have the universal appeal John Paul wishes his Church to achieve.

From *Redemptor Hominis*

The redeemer of man, Jesus Christ, is the center of the universe and of history. . . . He, the Son of the living God, speaks to people also as man: It is His life that speaks, His humanity, His fidelity to the truth, His all-embracing love. Furthermore, His death on the cross speaks—that is to say, the inscrutable depth of His suffering and abandonment. The Church never ceases to relive His death on the cross and His resurrection, which constitute the content of the Church's daily life. Indeed, it is by the command of the Christ Himself, her master, that the Church unceasingly celebrates the Eucharist, finding in it the "fountain of life and holiness," the efficacious sign of grace and reconciliation with God, and the pledge of eternal life. The Church lives His mystery, draws unwearyingly from it, and continually seeks ways of bringing this mystery of her master and lord to humanity—to the peoples, the nations, the succeeding generations, and every individual human being. . . . In the mystery of redemption, man becomes newly "expressed" and, in a way, is newly created. . . . The man who wishes to understand himself thoroughly must, with his unrest, uncertainty, and even his weakness and sinfulness, with his life and death, draw near to

Christ. He must, so to speak, enter into Him with all his own self, he must "appropriate" and assimilate the whole of the reality of the incarnation and redemption in order to find himself. . . .

Jesus Christ is the stable principle and fixed center of the mission that God Himself has entrusted to man. We must all share in this mission and concentrate all our forces on it, since it is more necessary than ever for mankind. If this mission seems to encounter greater opposition nowadays than ever before, this shows that today it is more necessary than ever and, in spite of the opposition, more awaited than ever. . . . Since man's true freedom is not found in everything that the various systems and individuals propagate as freedom, the Church, because of her divine mission, becomes all the more the guardian of this freedom, which is the condition and basis for the human person's true dignity. . . . Today, even after 2000 years, we see Christ as the one who brings man freedom based on truth, frees man from what curtails, diminishes, and, as it were, breaks off this freedom at its root, in man's soul, his heart, and his conscience. . . .

We are not dealing with the *abstract* man, but the real, *concrete, historical* man. We are dealing with "each" man, for each one is included in the mystery of the redemption and with each one Christ has united Himself forever through this mystery. Every man comes into the world through being born of his mother, and precisely on account of the mystery of the redemption is entrusted to the solicitude of the Church. Her solicitude is about the whole man and is focused on him in an altogether special manner. The object of her care is man in his unique, unrepeatable human reality, which keeps intact the image and likeness of God Himself. . . . This is man in all the fullness of the mystery in which he has become a sharer in Jesus Christ, the mystery in which each one of the four billion human beings living on our planet has become a sharer from the moment he is conceived beneath the heart of his mother. . . .

The man of today is afraid that what he produces can radically turn against him; he is afraid that it can become the means and instrument for an unimaginable self-destruction, compared with which all the cataclysms and catastrophes of history known to us seem to fade away. . . . The development of technology and the development of contemporary civilization, which is marked by the ascendancy of technology, demand a proportional development of morals and ethics. For the present, this last development seems unfortunately to be always left behind. . . . But the question keeps coming back with regard to what is most essential—whether in the context of his progress man, as man, is becoming truly better; that is to say, more mature spiritually, more aware of the dignity of his humanity, more responsible, more open to others, especially the neediest and the weakest, and readier to give and to aid all. . . .

Man cannot relinquish himself or the place in the visible world that belongs to him; he cannot become the slave of things, the slave of economic systems, the slave of production, the slave of his own products. A civilization purely materialistic condemns man to such slavery. . . . Everyone is familiar with the picture of the consumer civilization, which consists in a certain surplus of goods necessary for man and for entire societies, while the remaining societies are suffering from hunger, with many people dying each day of starvation and malnutrition. Hand in hand go a certain abuse of freedom by one group—an abuse linked precisely with a consumer attitude uncontrolled by ethics—and a limitation by it of the freedom of others, that is to say, those suffering marked shortages and being driven to conditions of even worse misery and destitution. . . . We have before us a great drama that can leave nobody indifferent. The person, who, on the one hand, is trying to draw the maximum profit, and, on the other hand, is paying the price in damage and injury, is always man. . . . Add to this the fever of inflation and the plague of unemployment—these are further symptoms of the moral disorder that is being noticed in the world situation and therefore requires daring creative resolves in keeping with man's authentic dignity. . . . This difficult road of the indispensable transformation of the structures of economic life is one on which it will not be easy to go forward without the intervention of a true conversion of mind, will, and heart. The task requires resolute commitment by individuals and nations that are free and linked in solidarity. . . .

The Church has always taught the duty to act for the common good and, in so doing, has likewise educated good citizens for each state. Furthermore, she has always taught that the fundamental duty of power is solicitude for the common good of society; this is what gives power its fundamental rights. Precisely in the name of these premises of the objective ethical order, the rights of power can only be understood on the basis of respect for the objective and inviolable rights of man. The common good that authority in the state serves is brought to full realization only when all citizens are sure of their rights. . . .

Seeking to see man, as it were, with "the eyes of Christ himself," the Church becomes more and more aware that she is the guardian of a great treasure, which she may not waste but must continually increase. . . . The Church is united with the Spirit of Christ, that Holy Spirit promised and continually communicated by the redeemer, and whose descent, which was revealed on the day of Pentecost, endures forever. This appeal to the Spirit, intended precisely to obtain the Spirit, is the answer to all the "materialisms" of our age. . . . The invocation to the Spirit to obtain the Spirit is really a constant self-insertion into the full magnitude of the mystery of the redemption in which Christ, united with the Father and with each man, continually communicates to us the Spirit who places within us the sentiments of the Son and directs us toward the Father. This is why the Church of our time—a time particularly hungry for the Spirit, because it is hungry for justice, peace, love, goodness, fortitude, responsibility, and human dignity—must concentrate and gather around that mystery, finding in it the light and the strength that are indispensable for her mission. . . .

Faith as a specific supernatural virtue infused into the human spirit makes us sharers in knowledge of God as a response to His revealed word. Therefore, it is required, when the Church professes and teaches the faith, that she should strictly adhere to divine truth. . . . A particular share in this office belongs to the pastors of the Church, who teach and continually and in various ways proclaim and transmit the doctrine concerning the Christian faith and morals. . . . And although we are speaking of priests here, we must also mention the great number of men and women religious dedicating themselves to catechetical activity for love of the divine master. Finally, it would be difficult not to mention the many lay people who find expression in this activity for their faith and their apostolic responsibility. . . .

The Church not only shares in the Gospel of her master through fidelity to the word and service of truth, but she also shares, through a submission filled with hope and love, in the power of His redeeming action expressed and enshrined by Him in a sacramental form, especially in the Eucharist. The Eucharist is the center and summit of the whole of sacramental life, through which each Christian receives the saving power of the redemption. . . . The Christ who calls to the Eucharistic banquet is always the same Christ who exhorts us to penance. . . . The sacrament of penance is the means to satisfy man with the righteousness that comes from the redeemer Himself. . . .

The full truth about human freedom is indelibly inscribed on the mystery of the redemption. The Church truly serves mankind when she guards this truth with untiring attention, fervent love, and mature commitment, and when in the whole of her community, she transmits it and gives it concrete form in human life through each Christian's fidelity to his vocation. . . .

Married people must be distinguished for fidelity for their vocation, as is demanded by the indissoluble nature of the sacramental institution of marriage. Priests must be distinguished for a similar fidelity to their vocation, in view of the indelible character that the Sacrament of Orders stamps on their souls. In receiving this sacrament, we in the Latin Church knowingly and freely commit ourselves to live in celibacy, and each one of us must do all he can, with God's grace, to be thankful for this gift and faithful to the bond that he has accepted forever. He must do so as married people must, for married people must endeavor with all their strength to persevere in their matrimonial union, building up the family community through this witness of love, and educating new generations of men and women, capable in their turn of dedicating the whole of their lives to their vocation, that is to say, to the *kingly service* of which Jesus Christ has offered us the example and the most beautiful model. . . .

The Church is a mother and, particularly in our time, has need of a mother. . . . If we feel a special need, in this difficult and responsible phase of the history of the Church and of mankind, to turn to Christ, who is Lord of the Church and Lord of man's history on account of the mystery of redemption, we believe that nobody else can bring us as Mary can into the divine and human dimension of this mystery. Nobody has been brought into it by God Himself as Mary has. The exceptional character of the grace of the divine motherhood consists in this.

6

To Be Fully Human: Pontifical Addresses and Homilies

When God asks "Where art Thou?"—be the question addressed to Adam or any other man—he does not expect to be told something he does not already know. But he does want something to take effect inside the man which only such a question can effect—provided the man lets his heart be moved by it.

MARTIN BUBER

JOHN Paul has spoken to the crowds in the Basilica and on St. Peter's Square whenever he was in Rome and has made the rounds of his bishopric. He has visited cities and villages in various parts of Italy. He has gone to his native Poland. He has been to Ireland, to Turkey, to Central and South America, to Africa, and to the United States.

Much of his time is taken up by ceremonials as head of state and by administrative matters as head of a far-flung bureaucracy. But, as public a figure as he is—mobbed and acclaimed—his words have consistently been those of a man who would try to reach the inner core of his every listener.

He wants agape *(love of mankind) to animate human action and yet he knows the reality of hate, terrorism, poverty and injustice, and the political structures that cause and perpetuate them. Whatever power he possesses by virtue of the office he holds, he can force no one—not even his own clergy—to listen to him or obey him unconditionally. But millions listen and millions do obey.*

As the selections from his statements, addresses and homilies show, Karol Wojtyla's views have not changed since his becoming Pope, nor has his basic purpose which is to teach and to offer guidance to those willing to accept it—believers and non-believers alike.

Advent—A Dimension of Life

How much food for thought there is in the behavior of the two young men to whom their father says, one after the other: "Son, go and work in the vineyard today" (Mt. 21:28). The first says he is ready and does not keep his word. The other, on the contrary, first says: "I will not," but he then goes and sets to work. When Christ asks: "Which of the two did the will of his father?" the answer comes spontaneously: obviously the latter.

Listening to these words, let us be ready to refer them to ourselves. We ask ourselves the question: Which of these two brothers do I resemble more? Which of their behavior does my usual behavior resemble? Am I one of those who get carried away easily, promise at once, and then do not keep his word? Or am I, rather, the man who first says "no"? This first "no," perhaps, has become even too much of a habit, almost a rule of my behavior. I say "no" not considering that I may harm someone with it. But . . . I need that "no" to be able to reflect, to meditate on the pros and cons in order, finally, to make a decision. And, as a result, after having first said "no," in the end I say "yes." Am I not, in this case, better than the one who, with his first "yes," had not done wrong, but who, in the end, did nothing? In the light of Christ's words, I have the right to think that my behavior is better. Each of us can develop such and similar meditations on his behavior. They are very useful. They are particularly useful for the young, who often ask themselves: Who am I? What am I like? What are my tendencies?

We have become accustomed to defining with the word *Advent* a certain liturgical period that precedes Christmas and prepares us for it. This liturgical *Advent*, in fact, is lived by us only to the extent to which we are capable of discovering *advent* in us as a fundamental dimension of our life, our earthly existence. And it is precisely to this that the owner of the vineyard calls his two sons.

What, in fact, does the *vineyard* mean? The *vineyard* is at once "inside us" and "outside us." We must cultivate, improving the world and improving ourselves. One depends on the other, in fact: I make the world better, to the extent that I improve myself. Otherwise, I am only a *technician* of the development of the world and not the *worker in the vineyard.* The first place of human existence was already this interior *vineyard.* We receive this interior *vineyard* in inheritance from the first man, just as we also inherit the exterior world, the earth that the Creator entrusted to man in order that he might subdue it.

At the same time, in the beginning, sin also enters man's history. Original sin is one of those realities over which the liturgy of Advent bends with particular attention. Against this background, we understand better the meaning of the feast of the Immaculate Conception which is celebrated in Advent. By stressing this exceptional privilege of the Virgin, chosen to become the mother of the redeemer, Advent wishes, at the same time, to remind us that this *vineyard,* inherited from our first ancestors, produces "thorns and thistles."

Who is Jesus Christ? The One for whose coming at night in Bethlehem we prepare, and every man prepares, by means of the liturgical period of Advent, which precedes the great festivity of Christmas? He is the full and definitive revelation of the advent of God in man's history. God, literally, comes to man. God comes to man in a radical and definitive way: He comes because of the fact that He Himself becomes man—the Son of man. He worked with human hands. He thought with a human mind, acted by human choice, and loved with a human heart. Born of the Virgin Mary, He has truly been made one of us, like us in all things except sin.

Jesus Christ is the most complete and definitive revelation of the advent of God in the history of mankind and in the history of every man, of each of us. And in Him, in His coming, in His birth in the stable in Bethlehem, then in His whole life and teaching, finally in His cross and His resurrection, we are called, one and all of us, definitively to the *vineyard.* He, who is the fullness of God's advent, is also the fullness of the divine call addressed to man.

Jesus was born in Bethlehem to reveal to us the truth of salvation and to bestow the life of grace on us! To live in grace is the supreme dignity. It is ineffable joy, it is a guarantee of peace, it is a marvelous ideal, and it must also be the logical concern of those who say they are followers of Christ.

Homily at Mass for Rome University Students in St. Peter's Basilica on 18 December 1979

Athletics

Athletic activity, if carried out according to correct criteria, aims at developing strength, skill, resistance, and balance in the organism, and at the same time encourages the growth of interior energies, becoming a school of loyalty, courage, endurance, resoluteness, and brotherhood.

Address to Italian and Argentine Football Teams on 25 May 1979

A Pilgrim at Auschwitz

On this site of the terrible slaughter that brought death to four million people of different nations, Father Maximilian Kolbe voluntarily offered himself for death in the starvation bunker for a brother, and so won a spiritual victory like that of Christ Himself. There is no doubt that many other similar victories were won. I am thinking, for example, of the death in the gas chamber of a concentration camp of the Carmelite Sister Benedicta of the Cross, whose name in the world was Edith Stein, who was an illustrious pupil of Husserl and became one of the glories of contemporary German philosophy, and who was a descendant of a Jewish family living in Wrocław. Where the dignity of man was so horribly trampled on, victory was won through faith and love.

I have come and I kneel on this Golgotha of the modern world, on these tombs, largely nameless like the great tomb of the Unknown Soldier. I kneel before all the inscriptions bewailing the memory of the victims of Oswiecim. In particular I pause before the inscription in Hebrew. This inscription awakens the memory of the people whose sons and daughters were intended for total extermination. This people draws its origin from Abraham, our father in faith, as was expressed by Paul of Tarsus. The very people that received from God the commandment "Thou shalt not kill," itself experienced in a special measure what is meant by killing. It is not permissible for anyone to pass by this inscription with indifference.

Finally, the last inscription: that in Polish. Six million Poles lost their lives during the Second World War: a fifth of the nation. This was yet another stage in the centuries-old fight of this nation, my nation, for its fundamental rights among the peoples of Europe; yet another loud cry for the right to a place of its own on the map of Europe; yet another painful reckoning with the conscience of mankind.

Oswiecim (Auschwitz) is such a reckoning. It is impossible merely to visit it. It is necessary on this occasion to think with fear of how far hatred can go, how far man's destruction of man can go, how far cruelty can go.

Oswiecim is a testimony of war. War brings a disproportionate growth of hatred, destruction, and cruelty. It cannot be denied that it also manifests new capabilities of human courage, heroism, and patriotism, but the fact remains that it is the reckoning of the losses that prevails. This reckoning prevails more and more, since each day sees an increase in the destructive capacity of the weapons invented by modern technology. Not only those who directly bring about wars are responsible for them, but also those who fail to do all they can to prevent them.

Therefore, I would like to repeat in this place the words that Paul VI pronounced before the United Nations organization: "It is enough to remember that the blood of millions of men, numberless and unprecedented sufferings, useless slaughter and frightful ruin are the sanction of the covenant that unites you in a solemn pledge that must change the future history of the world: No more war, war never again. It is peace, peace that must guide the destinies of nations and of all mankind."

He who is speaking these words is the successor of John XXIII and Paul VI. But he is also the son of a nation that in its history has suffered many afflictions from others. He says this, not to accuse but to remind. He is speaking in the name of all the nations whose rights are being violated and forgotten. He is saying it because he is urged to do so by the truth and by solicitude for man.

Homily at Open-Air Mass in Brzezinka (Birkenau) on 7 June 1979

Catechesis

The fundamental task of the Church is catechesis. In this work of an ever more conscious faith that is always newly introduced into the life of each generation, we know how much depends on the common effort of parents, of the family, of the parish, of the priests and pastors of souls, of men and women catechists, of the community, of the instruments of social communication and of customs.

In fact, the walls of the bell towers of the churches, the crosses at the crossroads, the holy pictures on the walls of the houses—all these, in a certain way, catechize. And on this great synthesis of the catechesis of life, in the present and in the past, depends the faith of future generations.

Address to the Population of Gniezno (Gnesen), Poland, on 3 June 1979

The Year of the Child

The Holy See thinks we can speak of the rights of the child from the moment of conception, and particularly of the right to life, for experience shows more and more that the child needs special protection even before his birth. Stress could thus be laid on the right of the child to be born in a real family, the parents remaining primarily and principally responsible for his education. The Church desires just as much to help form the conscience of men, to make public opinion aware of the child's essential rights.

Even the existence of wider family ties, with brothers and sisters, with grandparents, and other close relatives—which tends to be neglected today—is an important element for the child's harmonious balance.

In education, to which, together with the parents, the school and other organisms of society contribute, the child must find the possibilities "of developing in a healthy, normal way on the physical, intellectual, moral, spiritual, and social plane, in conditions of freedom and dignity."

The child also has the right to the truth, in teaching that takes into account the fundamental ethical values, and that will make possible a spiritual education, in conformity with the religion to which the child belongs, the orientation legitimately desired by his parents and the exigencies of freedom of conscience.

To speak of the rights of the child is to speak of the duties of parents and educators, who remain in the service of the child, of his higher interests. But the growing child must take part himself in his own development, with responsibilities that correspond to his capacities; and care must be taken not to neglect to speak to him also of his own duties toward others and toward society.

Address to European Journalists and Members of the Italian Commission for the International Year of the Child on 13 January 1979

Culture and Humanity

Culture is an expression of man, a confirmation of humanity. Man creates culture, and through culture creates himself. He creates himself with the inward effort of the spirit, of thought, will, and heart. At the same time, he creates culture in communion with others. Culture is an expression . . . of shared thought and collaboration by human beings. It is born of service to the common good and becomes an essential good of human communities.

Speech from the Balcony of the Archiepiscopal Residence on 3 June 1979

Einstein and the Immense Word

Scientific reason makes us rediscover things with new wonder. It induces us to raise again with renewed intensity some of the great questions of the man of always: Where do we come from? Where are we going? It leads us to pit ourselves once more against the frontiers of mystery, that mystery of which Einstein said that it is "the fundamental feeling that is at the side of the cradle of true art and true science" and, we add, of true metaphysics and true religion.

Is it not, fundamentally, a question of one great mystery: the one that is at the root of all things, of the cosmos and its origin, as well as of man who is capable of studying it and understanding it? If the universe is, as it were, an immense word that, though with difficulty and slowly, can at last be deciphered and understood, who is it who says this word to man?

Address to the Participants in the Conference on "The Problem of the Cosmos" in Honor of the Einstein Centenary on 28 September 1979

THE FAMILY

The deepest human problems are connected with the family. It constitutes the primary, fundamental, and irreplaceable community for man. The experience of the differrent nations in the history of mankind, as well as our contemporary experience, can serve to reaffirm that it is easy, in the fundamental sphere of human existence in which the role of the family is decisive, to destroy essential values, while it is very difficult to reconstruct these values.

The first of these values is the value of the person, which is expressed in absolute mutual faithfulness until death: the faithfulness of the husband to his wife and of the wife to her husband. The consequence of this affirmation of the value of the person, which is expressed in the mutual relationship between husband and wife, must also be respect for the personal value of the new life, that is, of the child, from the first moment of his conception.

Homily at the Celebration Dedicated to the Most Holy Name of Jesus on 31 December 1978

HUMAN RIGHTS

Humanity is divided in a great many ways. The search for solutions that will permit human societies to carry out their own tasks and to live in justice, is perhaps the main sign of our time.

The Church's mission is, by its very nature, religious, and consequently the meeting point of the Church or the Apostolic See with the multiform and differentiated life of the political communities of the modern world, is characterized particularly by the universally recognized principle of religious freedom and freedom of conscience. This principle is not only contained in the list of human rights admitted by everyone, but it has a key position on it. It is a question, in fact, of respect for a fundamental right of the human spirit, in which man expresses himself most deeply, perhaps, as man.

Address to the Diplomatic Corps on 12 January 1979

Varieties of Hunger

Widespread hunger remains today one of the telling signs of man's uncompleted quest for progress and for the mastery of creation. Millions of children are crying out to the world, pleading for food. And at the same time, millions of people are forced to bear in their bodies and their minds the results of a lack of proper nourishment when they were young. They exhibit before the witness of history the permanent scars of a diminished or severely handicapped physical and mental condition.

For all who are willing to see, hunger is so real; at the same time, hunger has so many facets. Man is hungry for food, and yet he realizes that he does not live "by bread alone." Man is also hungry for knowledge of the Creator, the giver of all good gifts; he hungers for love and truth. The human being hungers to be understood; he craves freedom and justice, and true and lasting peace.

Address to the Rotarians on 15 June 1979

Christians and Jews

Our two religious communities are connected and closely related at the very level of their respective religious identities. It is on the basis of this that we recognize with utmost clarity that the path along which we should proceed with the Jewish religious community is one of fraternal dialogue and fruitful collaboration.

The Holy See has sought to provide the instruments for such dialogue and collaboration, and to foster their realization both here at the center and elsewhere throughout the Church. Thus, the Commission for Religious Relations with the Jews was created in 1974. At the same time, the dialogue began to develop at several levels in the local Churches around the world and within the Holy See itself.

Both sides must continue their strong efforts to overcome the difficulties of the past, so as to fulfill God's commandment of love, and to sustain a truly fruitful and fraternal dialogue that contributes to the good of each of the partners involved and to our better service of humanity.

By pursuing this goal, we are all sure of being faithful and obedient to the will of God, the God of the patriarchs and prophets. All of us, Jews and Christians, pray frequently to him with the same prayers, taken from the book that we both consider to be the Word of God. It is for Him to give to both religious communities, so near to each other, that reconciliation and effective love that are, at the same time, His command and His gift. Each time that Jews recite the "Shema' Israel," each time that Christians recall the first and second commandments, we are, by God's grace, brought nearer to each other.

To the Presidents and Representatives of the Jewish World Organizations at an Audience on 12 March 1979

Liberation Theology

The *theology of liberation* is often connected (sometimes too exclusively) with Latin America; but it must be admitted that one of the great contemporary theologians, Hans Urs von Balthasar, is right when he demands a theology of liberation on a universal scale.

Liberation means man's inner transformation, which is a consequence of the knowledge of truth. Truth is important not only for the growth of human knowledge, deepening man's interior life in this way; truth also has a prophetic significance and power. As a prophet, as a witness to truth, Christ repeatedly opposes non-truth; He does so with great forcefulness.

This service of truth as participation in Christ's prophetic service is a task of the Church, which tries to carry it out in the various historical contexts. It is necessary to call by their name injustice, the exploitation of man by man, or the exploitation of man by the state, institutions, mechanisms of systems and regimes which sometimes operate without sensitivity. It is necessary to call by name every social injustice, discrimination, and violence inflicted on man against the body, against the spirit, against his conscience, and against his convictions.

Christ teaches us a special sensitivity for man, for the dignity of the human person, for human life, for the human spirit and body. It is this sensitivity which bears witness to knowledge of that truth "which makes us free." It is not permitted for man to conceal this truth from himself. It is not permitted to falsify it. It is not permitted to make this truth the object of a tender. It is necessary to speak of it clearly and simply, and not to condemn men, but to serve man's cause. Liberation also in the social sense begins with knowledge of the truth.

General Audience at the Vatican on 21 February 1979

Lent and Fasting

The Lenten time teaches us what must be the generous activity of the Christian in order that the spring of the spirit may occur, the blooming of good, the rising to new life with Jesus and in Jesus. The Church, a wise and loving mother, indicates suitable means to attain this admirable purpose. These are prayer, fasting, and alms giving. In prayer, one contacts and establishes a living and interesting dialogue with the Lord.

Fasting is the second element necessary for the spring of the spirit. More than mere abstinence from nourishment or material food, it represents a complex and deep reality. Fasting is a symbol, a sign, a serious and stimulating call to accept or to make renunciations. What renunciations? Renunciation of the "ego," that is, of so many caprices or unhealthy aspirations; renunciation of one's own defects, of impetuous passion, of unlawful desires. Fasting is being able to say "no," bluntly and firmly, to what is suggested or asked by pride, selfishness, and vice; listening to one's own conscience, respecting the good of others, remaining faithful to God's holy law.

Fasting means putting a limit on so many desires, sometimes good ones, in order to have full mastery of oneself, to learn to control one's own instincts, to train the will in good. Fasting, finally, means depriving oneself of something in order to meet the need of one's brother, becoming, in this way, an exercise of goodness, of charity.

Fasting, understood, put into practice, lived in this way, becomes repentance, that is, conversion to God. For it purifies the heart from so much dross of evil, beautifies the soul with virtues, trains the will to good, dilates the heart to receive the abundance of divine grace. In this conversion, faith becomes stronger, hope more joyful, and charity more active!

To Young People at the Weekly General Audience in St. Peter's Basilica on 21 March 1979

Loneliness

The world of today is in extreme need of sensitive and qualified educators, who will teach their pupils to overcome the sadness and sense of loneliness and lack of communication that torments so many young people and sometimes even destroys them.

Homily during Mass at Chiesa Nuova in Vallicella on 26 May 1979

The Functions of Management

The entrepreneur and managerial staff must do everything in their power to give a hearing to the voice of the workers in their employ and to understand their legitimate demands for justice and fairness, overcoming all selfish temptations to make the economic factor a law unto itself. Many conflicts and antagonisms between workers and employers often have their roots in the unproductive soil of the refusal to listen, rejection of dialogue, or undue postponement of it.

Many factory workers, if obliged to live fenced off, as it were, in an artificial atmosphere, run the risk of feeling atrophied in their interior spontaneity. The very relations between fellow workers, when they become depersonalized, cannot give the necessary comfort or support; and the machinery of production, distribution, and consumption often forces workers to live in a "standardized" way, without initiatives, without choices.

This level of dehumanization is reached when the scale of values is reversed and "productivism" becomes the only parameter of the industrial phenomenon, when the interior dimension of values is neglected, when the aim pursued is rather the perfection of the one who carries it out, giving preference to the work as compared with the worker, the object as compared with the subject.

Only in this perspective, man—every man, whether he is an entrepreneur or executive, or a collaborator in the various sectors, of the clerical class and workers—can find again his own deep meaning, thus being enabled to express his talents, collaborate, participate, and cooperate in the smooth operation of the enterprise, of which all are, together, collaborators and architects.

In this way, the time allotted for work also recovers its important meaning, no less than that reserved for rest. They both allow man to rediscover himself and at the same time rediscover those superior values of love and solidarity that allow him to reach complete development, freeing him of possible and ever imminent frustrations.

Address to Members of the Christian Union of Entrepreneurs and Managers on 24 November 1979

Children and the Media

Like soft wax on which every tiniest pressure leaves a mark, so the child is responsive to every stimulus that plays upon his imagination, his emotions, his instincts, and his ideas. Yet the impressions received at this age are the ones that are destined to penetrate most deeply into the psychology of the human being and to condition, often in a lasting way, the successive relationships with himself, with others, and with his environment.

Children have a need for help in their development toward maturity. It is on the adults that the duty falls—on the parents, the educators, the communications workers—and it is they, also, who have the capability of enabling the child to sort things out and find himself.

You especially who are engaged in the mass media stand by his side and help him find an answer to his quest for his identity and for his gradual entry into the human community.

In begging you to make this kind of human and *poetic* effort (*poetic* in its true meaning, as the creative capacity proper to art), I am implicitly asking you to relinquish to some extent your adherence to program planning geared to instant success and closely tied to maximum audience ratings. Is not the true work of art, perhaps, that which is born not from ambition to succeed, but from genuine ability and sure professional maturity? Do not exclude from your productions—I ask this of you as a brother—the opportunity to offer to the heart of the children a spiritual and religious invitation.

Message to the XIII World Day of Social Communications on 27 May 1979

Moral Values and the Law

Human values, moral values, are at the basis of everything. Law cannot set them aside, neither in its objectives nor in its means. The whole history of law shows that law loses its stability and its moral authority, that it is then tempted to make an increasing appeal to constraint and physical force, or, on the other hand, to renounce its responsibility—in favor of the unborn or the stability of marriage or, on the international plane, in favor of entire populations abandoned to oppression—whenever it ceases to search for the truth concerning man and allows itself to be bought off with some harmful form of relativism. This is a difficult search, a groping search, but a necessary search of which the jurist least of all may divest himself.

Address to Participants in the Ninth World Conference on Law on 24 September 1979

The Meaning of Passover

In the Old Testament, Passover meant the exodus from the "house of slavery" of Egypt and the passing over the Red Sea, under the special protection of the Lord God, toward the "Promised Land." The wandering lasted for forty years. In the New Testament, this historic Passover was accomplished in Christ during three days: from Thursday evening to the Sunday morning. And it means the passing through death to the resurrection, and, at the same time, the exodus from the slavery of sin toward participation in God's life by means of grace.

Christ is He who accepted the whole reality of human dying. And for that very reason He is the One who made a radical change in the way of understanding life. He showed that life is a passing over, not only to the limit of death, but to a new life. Thus, the cross became for us the supreme chair of the truth of God and of man. We must all be pupils—no matter what our age is—of this chair. Then we will understand that the cross is also the cradle of the new man.

Those who are this chair's pupils look at life in this way, perceive it in this way. And they teach it in this way to others. They imprint this meaning of life on the whole of temporal reality: on morality, creativity, culture, politics, economics. It has very often been affirmed—as, for example, the followers of Epicurus sustained in ancient times, and as some followers of Marx do in our times for other reasons—that this concept of life distracts man from temporal reality and that it cancels it in a certain sense. The truth is quite different. Only this conception of life gives full importance to all the problems of temporal reality. It opens the possibility of placing them fully in man's existence. And one thing is certain: This conception of life does not permit shutting man up in temporary things, it does not permit subordinating him completely to them. It decides his freedom.

Giving human life this *paschal* meaning, that is, that it is a passing over to freedom, Jesus Christ taught with His word and even more with His own example that this is a test. The concept of *test* is closely connected with the concept of responsibility. Both are addressed to our will, to our acts. It is necessary to undertake this test with all responsibility. It is at the same time a personal responsibility—for my life, for its future pattern, for its value—and also a social responsibility, for justice and peace, for the moral order of one's own native environment and of the whole of society. It is a responsibility for the real common good. A man who has such an awareness of the meaning of life does not destroy, but constructs the future. Christ teaches us this.

A great tension exists in the modern world. All things considered, this is a tension over the sense of human life, the meaning we can and must give to this life if it is to be worthy of man, if it is to be such that it is worth living. There also exist clear symptoms of moving away from these dimensions; in fact, materialism in different forms, inherited from the last centuries, is capable of coercing this meaning of life. But materialism does not form the deepest roots of European or world culture. It is not at all a correlative or a full expression of epistemological or ethical realism. Christ—allow me to put it in this way—is the greatest realist in the history of man. On the basis of this realism, Christ teaches that human life has a meaning insofar as it is a testimony of truth and love.

The causes of evil are not to be sought outside man, but first and foremost inside his heart; and the remedy also starts from the heart. Then Christians, through the sincerity of the commitment, must rebel against the leveling down of man and proclaim with their own lives the joy of true liberation from sin by means of Christ's forgiveness. The Church does not have a project of her own ready for the university, for society, but she has a project for man, for the new man, born again from grace. Find the interior truth of your consciences again. May the Holy Spirit grant you the grace of a sincere repentance, of a firm purpose of amendment, and of a sincere confession of sins. May He grant you deep spiritual joy.

Homily at Easter Mass for Rome University Students on 5 April 1979

The Power of Peace

It is a fact, and no one doubts it, that truth serves the cause of peace. It is also beyond discussion that nontruth in all its forms and at all levels (lies, partial or slanted information, sectarian propaganda, manipulation of the communications media, and so on) goes hand in hand with the cause of war.

Violence flourishes in lies, and needs lies. The first lie, the basic falsehood, is to refuse to believe in man, with all his capacity for greatness, but at the same time with his need to be redeemed from the evil and sin within him.

Encouraged by differing and often contradictory ideologies, the idea is spreading that the individual and all humanity achieve progress principally through violent struggle. It has become more and more the custom to analyze everything in social and international life exclusively in terms of relationships of power and to organize accordingly in order to impose one's own interests.

This widespread tendency to have recourse to trials of strength in order to make justice is often held in check by tactical or strategic pauses. But, as long as threats are permitted to remain, as long as selective support is given to certain forms of violence in line with interests or ideologies, as long as support is given to the claim that the advance of justice comes, in the final analysis, through violent struggle—as long as these things happen, then niceties, restraint, and selectivity will periodically give way in the face of the simple and brutal logic of violence, a logic that can go as far as the suicidal exaltation of violence for its own sake.

With minds so confused, building up peace by works of peace is difficult. Restoring peace means, in the first place, calling by their proper names acts of violence in all their forms. Murder must be called by its proper name: murder is murder; political or ideological motives do not change its nature, but are, on the contrary, degraded by it. The massacre of men and women, whatever their race, age, or position, must be called by its proper name. Torture must be called by its proper name; and, with the appropriate qualifications, so must all forms of oppression and exploitation of man by man, of man by the state, of one people by another people. The purpose of doing so is not to give oneself a clear conscience by means of loud all-embracing denunciations nor to brand and condemn individuals and peoples, but to help change people's behavior and attitudes, and to give peace a chance again.

To promote truth as the power of peace means that we ourselves must make a constant effort not to use the weapons of falsehood, even for a good purpose. Falsehood can cunningly creep in anywhere. If sincerity—truth with ourselves—is to be securely maintained, we must make a patient and courageous effort to seek and find the higher and universal truth about man, in the light of which we will first judge ourselves and our own sincerity.

One of violence's lies is to try to justify itself by systematically and radically discrediting opponents, their actions, and the social and ideological structures within which they act and think. But the man of peace is able to detect the portion of truth existing in every human undertaking and, moreover, to discern the capacity for truth to be found within every human being. Truth does not allow us to despair of our opponents. The man of peace inspired by truth does not equate his opponent with the error into which he sees him fall. One of the big lies that poison relations between individuals and groups consists in ignoring all aspects of an opponent's action, even the good and just ones, for the sake of condemning him more completely. Truth follows a different path; this is why truth does not throw away any of the chances of peace.

Above all, truth gives us all the more reason not to despair of the victims of injustice. It does not allow us to drive them to the despair of resignation or violence. It encourages us to count on the forces for peace that suffering individuals or peoples have deep within them. It believes that by confirming them in awareness of their dignity and inalienable rights it gives them the strength to exercise upon the forces of oppression effective pressure for transformation, pressure more effective than acts of violence, which generally lack any future prospect—except one of greater suffering.

There is no peace without readiness for sincere and continual dialogue. Truth causes minds to come together; it shows what already unites the parties that were previously opposed; it causes the mistrust of yesterday to decrease, and prepares the ground for fresh advances in justice and brotherhood and in the peaceful coexistence of all human beings.

The situation in which humanity is living today seems to include a tragic contradiction between the many fervent declarations in favor of peace and the no less vertiginous escalation in weaponry. The very existence of the arms race can even cast a suspicion of falsehood and hypocrisy on certain declarations of the desire for peaceful coexistence. What is worse, it can often even justify the impression that such declarations serve only as a cloak for opposite intentions.

We cannot sincerely condemn recourse to violence unless we engage in a corresponding effort to replace it by courageous political initiatives that aim at eliminating threats to peace by attacking the roots of injustice. The profound truth of politics is contradicted just as much when it settles into passivity as when it hardens and degenerates into violence. Promoting the truth that gives strength to peace in politics means having the courage to detect in good time latent conflicts and to reexamine at suitable moments problems that have been temporarily defused by laws or agreements that have prevented them from getting worse. Promoting truth also means having the courage to foresee the future: to take into account the new aspirations, compatible with what is good, that individuals and peoples begin to experience as culture progresses, in order to adjust national and international institutions to the reality of humanity on the march.

Statesmen and international institutions, therefore, have an immense field for building a new and more just world order, based on the truth about man and established upon a just distribution not only of wealth but also of power and responsibility.

Jesus revealed to man the full truth about man; He restores man in the truth about himself by reconciling him with God, by reconciling him with himself, and by reconciling him with others. Truth is the driving power of peace because it reveals and brings about the unity of man with God, with himself, and with others. Forgiveness and reconciliation are constitutive elements of the truth that strengthens peace and that builds up peace. To refuse forgiveness and reconciliation is for us to lie and to enter into the murderous logic of falsehood. All men and women of good will can understand this from personal experience, when they listen to the profound voice of their hearts.

Message for the World Day of Peace, 1 January 1980

A Word to the Peasants

In the depressed rural world, the worker, who with his sweat waters also his affliction, cannot wait any longer for full and effective recognition of his dignity, which is not inferior to that of any other social sector. He has the right to be respected and not to be deprived, with maneuvers that are sometimes tantamount to real spoliation, of the little he has. He has the right to be rid of the barriers of exploitation, often made up of intolerable selfishness, against which his best efforts of advancement are shattered. He has the right to real help—which is not charity or crumbs of justice—in order that he may have access to the development that his dignity as a man and as a son of God deserves.

Address to the Indios at Cuilapan, Mexico, on 29 January 1979

The Priesthood

Priestly life is built upon the foundation of the Sacrament of Orders, which imprints on our soul the mark of an indelible character. The priestly personality must be for others a clear and plain sign and indication. This is the first condition for our pastoral service. The people from among whom we have been chosen and for whom we have been appointed want above all to see in us such a sign and indication, and to this they have a right. It may sometimes seem to us that they do not want this or that they wish us to be in every way "like them." Here one very much needs a profound *sense of faith* and *the gift of discernment.*

Those who call for the secularization of priestly life and applaud its various manifestations will undoubtedly abandon us when we succumb to temptation. We shall then cease to be necessary and popular. Our time is characterized by different forms of *manipulation* and *exploitation* of man, but we cannot give in to any of these. In practical terms, the only priest who will always prove necessary to people is the priest who is conscious of the full meaning of his priesthood; the priest who believes profoundly, who professes his faith with courage, who prays fervently, who teaches with deep conviction, who serves, who puts into practice in his own life the program of the beatitudes, who knows how to love disinterestedly, who is close to everyone, and especially to those who are most in need.

Our pastoral activity demands that we should be close to people and all their problems, whether these problems be personal, family, or social ones, but it also demands that we should be close to all these problems *in a priestly way.* Only then do we remain ourselves. Therefore, if we are really of assistance in those human problems, and they are sometimes very difficult ones, then we keep our identity and are really faithful to our vocation. With great perspicacity we must seek, together with all men, truth and justice, the true and definitive dimension of which we can only find in the Gospel, or rather in Christ Himself. Our task is to serve truth and justice in the dimensions of human *temporality* but always in a perspective that is the perspective of eternal salvation.

The pastoral vocation of priests is great, and the Council teaches that it is universal: It is directed toward the whole Church, and therefore it is of a missionary character. Normally, it is linked to the service of a particular community of the people of God, in which each individual expects attention, care, and love. The heart of the priest, in order that it may be available for this service, must be free. Celibacy is a sign of a freedom that exists for the sake of service.

Every Christian who receives the Sacrament of Orders commits himself to celibacy with full awareness and freedom, after a training lasting a number of years, and after profound reflection and assiduous prayer. He decides upon a life of celibacy only after he has reached a firm conviction that Christ is giving him this *gift* for the good of the Church and the service of others. Only then does he commit himself to observe celibacy for his entire life. It is obvious that such a decision obliges not only by virtue of a law laid down by the Church but also by virtue of personal responsibility. It is a matter here of keeping one's word to Christ and the Church.

Keeping one's word is, at one and the same time, a duty and a proof of the priest's inner maturity; it is the expression of his personal dignity. It is shown in all its clarity when this keeping one's promise to Christ, made through a conscious and free commitment to celibacy for the whole of one's life, encounters difficulties, is put to the test, or is exposed to temptation—all things that do not spare the priest any more than they spare any other Christian. At such a moment, the individual must seek support in more fervent prayer. Through prayer, he must find within himself that attitude of humility and sincerity before God and his own conscience. Prayer helps us always to find the light that has led us since the beginning of our priestly vocation, and which never ceases to lead us, even though it seems at times to disappear in the darkness.

Prayer enables us to be converted continually, to remain in a state of continuous reaching out to God, which is essential if we wish to lead others to Him. Prayer helps us to believe, to hope, and to love, even when our human weakness hinders us.

Prayer likewise enables us continually to rediscover the dimensions of that kingdom for whose coming we pray every day, when we repeat the words Christ taught us.

Letter to All Bishops of the Church
on Holy Thursday 1979

The Problems of Science

The scientist discovers the still unknown energies of the universe and puts them in man's service. Through his work, he must therefore cause man and nature to grow at the same time. He must humanize man more, while respecting and perfecting nature. The universe has a harmony in all its parts, and every ecological imbalance leads to harm for man. So, the scientist will not treat nature as a slave, but he will consider it rather as a sister called to cooperate with him to open new ways for the progress of humanity.

This way cannot be traversed, however, without the help of technique, of technology that makes scientific research efficient.

There is no doubt that from many points of view technical

progress, born from scientific discoveries, helps man to solve very serious problems, such as food, energy, the struggle against certain diseases more than ever widespread in the Third World countries. But it is also true that man today is the victim of great fear, as if he were threatened by what he produces, by the results of his work and the use made of it. In order to prevent science and technique from becoming slaves to the will for power of tyrannical forces, political as well as economic, and in order positively to ordain science and technique to the advantage of man, what is necessary is a supplement of soul, a new breath of spirit, faithfulness to the moral norms that regulate man's life.

There is a link between faith and science. The Magisterium of the Church has always said so, and one of the founders of modern science, Galileo, wrote that "Holy Scripture and Nature both proceed from the divine Word: one, as being dictated by the Holy Spirit, and the other, as the very faithful executor of God's orders."

When scientists advance humbly in their search for the secrets of nature, God's hand leads them toward the summits of the mind. Faith does not offer resources to scientific research as such, but it encourages the scientist to pursue his research knowing that he meets, in nature, the presence of the Creator.

Pure science is a good, which every nation must be able to cultivate in full freedom from all forms of international slavery or intellectual colonialism. Basic research must be free with regard to the political and economic authorities, which must cooperate in its development, without hampering it in its creativity or harnessing it to serve their own purposes. Like any other truth, scientific truth is answerable only to itself and to the supreme truth, God, the Creator of man and of all things.

Science turns to practical applications, which find their full development in the various technologies. In the phase of its concrete achievements, science is necessary to mankind to satisfy the rightful requirements of life, and to overcome the different ills that threaten it. There is no doubt that applied science has rendered and will continue to render immense services to man, provided it is inspired by love, regulated by wisdom, and accompanied by the courage that defends it against the undue interference of tyrannical powers. Applied science must be united with conscience, so that, in the trinomial science-technology-conscience, it is the cause of man's real good that is served.

Address to Members of the European Physical Society on 30 March 1979
Address to Pontifical Academy of Sciences on 10 November 1979

Ministering to the Sick

Jesus, who is present in our suffering neighbor, wishes to be present in every act of charity and service of ours, which is expressed also in every glass of water we give in His name. Jesus wants love, the solidarity of love, to grow from suffering and around suffering. He wants, that is, the sum of that good which is possible in our human world; a good that never passes away.

The Pope, who wishes to be a servant of this love, kisses the forehead and kisses the hands of all those who contribute to the presence of this love and to its growth in our world. He knows, in fact, and believes that he is kissing the hands and the forehead of Christ Himself, who is mystically present in those who suffer and in those who, out of love, serve the suffering.

Homily at Mass for the Sick of UNITALSI on 11 February 1979

Dialogue with the Sister Church

For nearly a whole millennium, the two sister Churches grew side by side, as two great vital and complementary traditions of the same Church of Christ, keeping not only peaceful and fruitful relations, but also concern for the indispensable communion in faith, prayer, and charity, which they did not at any cost want to question, despite their different sensitivity. The second millennium, on the contrary, was darkened, apart from some fleeting intervals of light, by the distance that the two Churches put between each other, with all the fatal consequences thereof.

The wound is not yet healed. But the Lord can cure it, and he bids us do our best to help the process. Here we are now at the end of the second millennium: Is it not time to hasten toward perfect brotherly reconciliation, so that the dawn of the third millennium may find us standing side by side, in full communion, to bear witness together to salvation before the world, the evangelization of which is waiting for this sign of unity?

With realism and wisdom it has been decided to reestablish relations and contacts between the Catholic Church and the Orthodox Churches, which would make it possible to recognize each other and to create the atmosphere necessary for a fruitful theological dialogue.

This period has rightly been called the dialogue of charity. This dialogue has made it possible to become aware again of the deep communion that already unites us, and enables us to consider each other and treat each other as sister Churches. A great deal has already been done, but this effort must be continued. It is necessary to draw the consequences of this mutual theological rediscovery, wherever Catholics and Orthodox live together. Habits of isolation must be overcome in order to collaborate in all fields of pastoral action in which this collaboration is made possible by the almost complete communion that already exists between us.

We must not be afraid to reconsider, on both sides and in consultation with one another, canonical rules established when awareness of our communion was still dimmed, rules that, perhaps, no longer correspond to the results of the dialogue of charity and to the possibilities they have opened.

This theological dialogue that is about to begin now will have the task of overcoming the misunderstandings and disagreements that still exist between us, if not at the level of faith, at least at the level of theological formulation. It should take place not only in the atmosphere of the dialogue of charity, which must be developed and intensified, but also in an atmosphere of worship and availability.

The question we must ask ourselves is not so much whether we still have the right to remain separated. We must ask ourselves this question in the name of our faithfulness to Christ's will for His Church, for which constant prayer must make us both more and more available in the course of the theological dialogue.

Discourse at the Greek Orthodox Cathedral of St. George at Phanar, Turkey, on 30 November 1979 mother of the Church." "From the moment of the *fiat*"—St. Anelm remarks—"Mary began to bear us all in her womb." From the ioment when the Virgin becomes mother of the incarnate Word, ie Church is constituted secretly, but perfectly in its germ, in its ssence as the mystical body: There are present, in fact, the reeemer and the first of the redeemed. Henceforth, incorporation ito Christ will involve a filial relationship not only with the heavnly Father, but also with Mary, the earthly mother of the Son of iod.

Every mother transmits to her children her own resemblance; ius there is a relationship of deep resemblance between Mary and ie Church. The transition from the old to the new people of God, om Israel to the Church, is made in her. She is the first among the umble and the poor who have remained faithful, and who are vaiting for redemption. She is again the first among the redeemed vho, in humility and obedience, welcome the coming of the reeemer. Eastern theology has laid great stress on the *katharsis* that akes place in Mary at the moment of the Annunciation.

In the liturgy in which the Eastern Church celebrates the praises f the Virgin, there is a special place for the canticle that Mary, the ister of Moses, sings at the crossing of the Red Sea, as if to signify hat the Virgin was the first to cross the waters of sin, at the head of he new people of God, liberated by Christ. Mary is the first fruit nd the most perfect image of the Church. Mary remains in the eyes f all believers as the entirely pure, entirely beautiful, entirely holy reature, capable "of being the Church" as no other creature will ver be here below.

Mary lived her faith in an attitude of continual deepening and rogressive discovery, going through difficult moments of darkness, eginning with the first days of her pregnancy, moments that she vercame thanks to a responsible attitude of listening and obedience o the Word of God.

Mary presents herself to us as an example of courageous hope and ctive charity: She walked in hope with docile readiness, passing rom Jewish hope to Christian hope, and she lived in charity by acepting in herself all its demands up to the most complete donation nd the greatest sacrifice. Faithful to her example, we too must reiain firm in hope, even when storm clouds gather over the Church, vhich advances like a ship in the midst of the often unfavorable bil-

The Theologian's Task

The humility of which the greatest masters of tl such a splendid example, is accompanied by deep ; can one fail to be grateful when the infinite God speak to man in His own human language?

How can we fail to be grateful when, in this w guage and human thought were visited by the Word divine truth and were called to participate in it, to be and to proclaim it and also explain it and study it d corresponding to the possibilities and requireme knowledge? This is precisely what theology is. Tl what the vocation of the theologian is.

Humility suggests to the theologian the right attitu to the Church. He does not let himself be shut up in of her particular and contingent historical expressic that the Church is a living mystery and on her way, ance of the Spirit. Likewise, he rejects proposals of with what has existed, on account of the fascinating beginning: He believes that Christ is always present today as yesterday, in order to continue her life, no over again.

Homily to Recto
Students of the
Universities and
leges of Rome in
ica on 15 October

The Virgin Mary

God does not impose salvation. Nor did He impose the case of the Annunciation, He turns to her in a pe peals to her will, and waits for an answer that will s faith. In this way the *fiat* of the Annunciation opens nant between God and His creature. While this *fi* Jesus in our stock according to human nature, it inco in Jesus according to the order of grace. The bond bet mankind, broken by sin, is now happily reestablishe

Uttering her *fiat*, Mary does not just become mothe ical Christ; her gesture sets her as mother of the t lows of the events of this world. We too must grow in charity, developing humility, poverty, availability, the ability to listen and be attentive, adhering to what she taught us by the witness of her whole life.

Homily at Open-Air Mass in Ephesus on 30 November 1979

WOMEN AND THE CHURCH

Modern society in which we live and work is suffering from a crisis of growth. On the one hand, it offers encouraging examples of renewed striving towards goals of justice, mutual communion, and a higher human level of life. The sense of solidarity and interdependence is growing, together with a healthy demand for respect of one's own identity and one's own values. Yet, on the other hand, irrational manifestations of selfishness that reach the point of licentiousness and violence are not rare. Forces that aim at the disintegration of the connecting tissues of society are operating with success, and forms of so-called reappropriation of life, which lead to one's own destruction and that of others, are exalted.

We are confronted with generosity ruined by pride, forms of real altruism coexisting with unbridled individualism, acclamation of resolutions in defense of life, and even of ecology, in blatant association with real attempts to humiliate and suffocate it.

In such a society, the Church has a precise function, to stimulate orderly and complete growth toward her full maturity. In this delicate but decisive process, the Church recognizes women's contribution as an essential one. She expects of them unmistakable commitment and witness in favor of all that founds and constitutes man's true dignity, his success at the personal and community level, and therefore his deepest happiness.

Women, in fact, have from God their own native charism, made up of keen sensitivity and a delicate perception of measure, a sense of the concrete and of providential love for what is in the germinal state and therefore in need of thoughtful care.

The world of women itself needs the healthy and balanced model of a complete woman. It is a question of asserting just rights, so that every woman can honestly take her place in society, both on the human and the professional plane, beyond all fear and discrimination. But care must also be taken not to allow claims and proposals, which are perfectly just at the outset, to make way subsequently for degenerated forms of exasperated polemics or arbitrary and unnatural proclamation. It is not lawful to introduce elements of rupture where the Creator envisaged and willed the highest harmony on the human plane.

The law should be not a mere recording of what is happening, but a model and stimulus for what must be done. The Church is deeply convinced that the wisdom of a legislation is shown most where the most energetic defense of the weakest and most helpless members is assumed, from the first moments of life. Therefore, any yielding in this matter is bound to be to the detriment of human dignity itself. And furthermore, while with respect and even with love for everyone, care must be taken not to adopt compromising positions of acceptance of ideological forces in conflict with the Christian faith. Among the weakest members of society are also children, the sick, the old, the unemployed, the uneducated, and in general all those who are exposed to various forms of exploitation and abuse. One thing is certain: There is also a Christian consistency in public life; a Christian must always be a Christian, at all levels, without wavering, without giving way; in deeds, and not just in name.

To Participants in the XIX National Congress of the Italian Women's Center on 7 December 1979

The Working Class

Those who have the fortune to work, wish to do so in more human and secure conditions, to participate more justly in the fruit of the common effort as regards wages, social insurances, and the possibilities of cultural and spiritual development. They want to be treated as free and responsible men, called to take part in the decisions that concern their lives and their future. It is their fundamental right freely to create organizations to defend and promote their own interests and to contribute responsibly to the common good. The task is complicated today by the world economic crisis, the disorder of unjust commercial and financial circles, the rapid exhaustion of some resources, and the risks of irreversible contamination of the biophysical environment.

If mankind wishes to control an evolution that is slipping from its hand, if it wants to avoid the materialistic temptation that is gaining ground in a desperate flight forward, if it wants to ensure true development for men and for peoples, it must radically revise the concepts of progress that, under different names, have let spiritual values waste away.

The Church offers her aid. She keeps her essential energies to help men and human groups, contractors and workers, in order that they may become aware of the immense reserves of goodness they have within them, which they have already caused to yield fruit in their history, and which must give new fruit today.

The working class movement, to which the Church and Christians have made an original and different contribution, claims its rightful share of responsibility in the construction of a new world order. It has gathered the common aspirations of freedom and dignity. It has developed the values of solidarity, brotherhood, and friendship. In the experience of sharing, it has brought forth original forms of organizations, substantially improving the fate of many workers and contributing to making a mark in the industrial world.

The Church wishes to draw attention to a serious phenomenon that is very topical: the problem of migrant workers. We cannot close our eyes to the situation of millions of men who, in their search for work and for livelihood, have to leave their country and often their family. They have to cope with the difficulties of a new environment that is not always pleasant and welcoming, an unknown language and general conditions that plunge them into solitude and sometimes social exclusion for themselves and for their wives and children; even when advantage is not taken of these circumstances to offer lower wages, to reduce social insurance and welfare benefits, and to give housing conditions unworthy of a human being.

There are occasions on which the principle put into practice is that of obtaining the maximum performance from the emigrant worker without looking to the person. Faced with this phenomenon, the Church continues to proclaim that the principle to follow in this, as in other fields, is not that of allowing economic, social, and political factors to prevail over man, but, on the contrary, for the dignity of the human person to be put above everything else, and for the rest to be conditioned by it.

We would create a world unpleasant to live in, if we aimed only at having more, and did not think first and foremost of the person of the worker, his conditions as a human being and a son of God who is called to an eternal vocation, if we did not think of helping him to be more.

Address to Workers at Monterrey, Mexico, on 31 January 1979